A PROTESTANT STUDENT LEADER; A PRODUCT OF MODERN
MISSIONS IN MEXICO

Young Mexico is looking to the United States to-day
for friendship and help.

MODERN MISSIONS
IN MEXICO

BY

W. REGINALD WHEELER
DWIGHT H. DAY
JAMES B. RODGERS

———

PHILADELPHIA
THE WESTMINSTER PRESS
1925

Copyright, 1925, by the
Board of Christian Education of the
Presbyterian Church in the U.S.A.

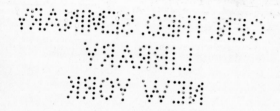
PRINTED IN THE UNITED STATES OF AMERICA

CONTENTS

iii

ILLUSTRATIONS

INTRODUCTION

THE present volume is the outgrowth of a two months' trip to Mexico to visit the Presbyterian Missions in that country.

The trip originated in the practice of the Foreign Mission Boards and Societies of sending, at stated intervals, commissions or deputations to visit the Missions on the field and to bring to the United States direct word about them to those interested. The particular Mission Board with whose work this book is concerned has approved of such a visitation for each of its Missions at least once in every seven years. In 1922–1923, Mexico, Colombia, and Venezuela were thus visited. In this book the work in Mexico is described; another volume, entitled *Modern Missions on the Spanish Main,* is devoted to Colombia and Venezuela.

The Commission in Mexico was composed of Dwight H. Day, Treasurer of the Presbyterian Board of Foreign Missions from 1906 to 1924; Dr. James B. Rodgers, who has spent ten years in Brazil and twenty-five years in the Philippines, where he was the founder of our Presbyterian Mission; and the Executive Secretary of the Presbyterian Foreign Board for its Latin American Missions.

The Commission crossed the Mexican border at Laredo, October 20, 1922, and spent two months in Mexico, sailing from Progreso, a southeastern port on the Yucatan peninsula, on December 18. During this time we traveled from the northern boundary to within twenty miles of the Guatemalan line on the south, from the Atlantic to the Pacific, traversing twelve of the twenty-eight states of Mexico, and visiting fifteen cities and towns. In the latter part of November and early in December, the Commission joined in the Jubilee services that celebrated the fiftieth anniversary of the founding of our Church in Mexico; later we met with the Mexico Mission in its annual meeting; and after several days in Yucatan, on December 18, sailed for Havana. From this port Dr. Rodgers and Mr. Day departed for New York, and the writer sailed for Panama and the South, where as a member of another Commission he was to visit the Missions in Colombia and Venezuela.

The first half of the volume was written while the Commission was in Mexico; chapters written during the trip have been left practically unchanged. Major changes in the local situation and progress since made in reaching objectives outlined in the earlier chapters are summarized in Chapter XXI. Mr. Day is chiefly responsible for Chapter VII, " Some Impressions of the Present Political and Economic Situation in Mexico," and Chapter XVIII, " The Constitution of 1917 and Property Holdings of Missions and Churches," as is Dr. Rodgers for Chapter XIV, " Remaking the Missionary Map of Mexico," and Chapter XV, " Progress and Problems in Protestant Coöperation." Dr. Moisés Saenz, First Assistant in the Department of Education in Mexico, has kindly written the section on " Public Education in Mexico," in Chapter XIX, and Rev. José Coffin has supplied the material for Chapter IX, " A Mexican's View of a Pioneer Protestant Church in Southern Mexico." For the rest of the book the writer is responsible. The volume as a whole could not have been produced without the help and guidance of the various members of the Mexico Mission and the Commission is grateful for their kind cooperation. We wish also to thank Miss Augustine Schafer and Miss Mabel V. Schluter for their assistance in preparing the manuscript and seeing the volume through the press, and the Westminster Press for coöperating in the publication of the book and for many courtesies during its preparation.

The Commission wishes to call attention to a volume entitled *Report on India and Persia,* by Dr. Robert E. Speer and Russell Carter, which contains a thorough study of Presbyterian Missions and of their environment in India and Persia, prepared during and after the visit of a Commission to those countries in 1921 and 1922. To these studies of modern missions on the other side of the world, the authors of the present volume are indebted for guidance and inspiration in preparing this book.

Where property and equipment are mentioned in this volume, with suggestions as to additional items needed, the fact should be kept clear that the views presented are those of the Commission, and do not necessarily represent the most recent actions of Mission and Board. These latter are of course the only actions that are " official," and they should be secured by individuals who are interested in such matters.

In conclusion, the Commission desires to express its warm gratitude for the innumerable kindnesses of the members of the Missions visited and of many friends along the way. " We had happy meetings with the missionaries of various denominations, inspecting their work in their company, and some of them entertained us with such generosity and even sacrifice as could spring only from hearts dominated by the utmost good will and brotherliness." " Mexico seems destined by Nature to be loved as fervently as ever any land is loved " and we shared in this feeling for this picturesque, beautiful, and uniquely interesting country. No one can be with our missionaries there and know their problems and trials and triumphs without feeling the warmest affection and admiration for them, and the deep desire to serve them. There are passages in the New Testament which have had a much deeper meaning since our visit to Mexico. We have seen and talked with men who bear about in their bodies the marks of the Lord Jesus. Verses from the seventh chapter of The Acts apply truly to scenes being enacted in Mexico to-day: " And they stoned " Alfonso, or Feliciano, or Fernando, " calling upon the Lord, and saying, Lord Jesus, receive my spirit. And he kneeled down, and cried with a loud voice, Lord, lay not this sin to their

charge. And when he had said this, he fell asleep."
Throughout the history of the Protestant movement, and even within recent months, there have
been Mexican disciples of the Master who have
thus fallen asleep in Him, and in Mexico, as in
other lands, the blood of the martyrs has been the
seed of the Church. No one can associate with the
members of our Church and of the other Protestant Churches, and learn the record of their progress against such heavy odds, or come to know the
people of Mexico as a whole, without realizing that
in that great multitude which no man can number,
who have come out of great tribulation and now
stand before the throne on high, are those from
Mexico who by faithfulness even unto death have
won a place in that celestial throng; and that here
and now on our own national borders are a people
and a Church who are entitled to that high comradeship and association of helpfulness that Jesus
meant when He said that we should love our neighbors as ourselves.

W. REGINALD WHEELER

156 FIFTH AVENUE,
NEW YORK CITY

CHAPTER I

FIRST IMPRESSIONS OF MEXICO

PUEBLA, MEXICO,
November 2, 1922

ON October 20, we crossed the border at Laredo. During the past twelve days we have visited the cities of Monterey, Saltillo, San Luis Potosí, Aguascalientes, Zacatecas, Mexico City and the Federal District, and Puebla. We have attended meetings of the local churches and have conferred with their representatives in each of these cities. In my next letter I will try to summarize some of our experiences in these conferences and meetings; this letter will carry to you our general impressions of the land and the people.

When we crossed the international border at Laredo, we were at once impressed by the pains taken by the government to keep peace within the state. Our baggage was carefully searched for arms, ammunition, and other contraband; heavily armed guards were on board our train. The inspection of our trunks was most thorough, the officials investigating even the toes of the shoes packed therein and unrolling blankets and duffle bags. Various books were in my trunk; the inspector paused for some time before one entitled *The Conquest of New Granada,* the cover of which

1

was profusely decorated with swords. On the train the inspection was repeated. One Mexican gentleman was forced to hand over temporarily a revolver and ammunition which he had concealed in his overcoat. On the trains were guards armed with revolvers and rifles. Part of the time these soldiers rode as lookouts on the tops of the cars, where, with their sombreros and their slung rifles, they made picturesque silhouettes against the clear Mexican sky. In spite of, or perhaps because of, the military atmosphere and precautions, our journey has been most peaceful thus far, and the indications are that President Obregon has the general support of the people in his program of peace and reconstruction.

The people of Mexico have an extraordinarily diverse racial background. Approximately ten per cent are of pure Spanish and European blood; fifty per cent are of pure Indian stock; the remaining forty per cent are of mixed race. In appearance many of these contrasted types are most picturesque. We have seen individuals who apparently were pure-blooded Spaniards, with dark mustaches and eyes and thin faces as in a Velásquez portrait. Such an individual, when on horseback, with silver-mounted stirrups and bridle chains, presents a most impressive figure — a true *caballero* of the Conquest transported to the twentieth century. More numerous are the Indians — the women blanketed and often carrying bundles or baskets on their heads; the men in towering sombreros, muffled in serapes, or blankets, as Remington has so often pictured them. " Occasionally among these Indians one sees a face so beautiful that one might suppose such another was the Indian who enchanted Cortes; with eyes and hair of extraordinary beauty, a complexion dark but glowing, with the Indian beauty of teeth like the driven snow." Then there are the mestizos and others of mixed parentage. The students in a school present startling contrasts, especially from the standpoint of one who has come from the Orient where all the faces are so homogeneous and so impassively self-controlled. Here are boys and girls with dark eyes and dark hair and others with blue eyes and fair complexions; here, too, are dark-skinned Indians and ruddy Europeans, the stoical calm of the Indian contrasting with the mobility of feature and the scarcely veiled emotionalism of the Latin.

The natural beauty of the country has also impressed us. The northern and central portion of Mexico, where we have traveled thus far, is a huge table-land with an average elevation of 6,000 feet above sea level; mountain ranges averaging 9,000 feet in height run north and south on this plateau. The country in general resembles New Mexico and California, though the mountains are more precipitous and sharply cut, and in the valleys and on the plateaus there is less irrigation with its consequent vegetation. Every city which we have visited has been hemmed in by a veritable mountain rampart, as a Chinese city is encircled by its ancient walls. The evening in Mexico City when we first saw Popocatepetl and Iztaccihuatl was memorable. These great peaks had been hidden by clouds until sunset. We climbed to the roof of one of the city buildings and looked out toward the encircling chain of mountains that marked the horizon to the north, west, and south. Lake Texcoco shone in the northeast distance. Over the western hills the sun was setting in a glory of gold. Then as we turned to the east we saw the towering peaks of "Old Popo" and of Iztaccihuatl — the one a pyramidal cone crowned with snow, gleaming like silver in the rays of the setting sun, the other a great white shoulder bulking massively against the darkening sky. Memories of Fujiyama and of the Jungfrau seen for the first time at just such an evening hour came back to me; the brown hills encircling the city recalled the Sierra Madre as they rise above Pasadena; here, were the grandeur and beauty of Japan and Switzerland and California all in one place and at one time.

In addition to the visible attempts to maintain political and military stability, to the racial diversity of the people, and to the beauty of the natural scenery, we noticed especially the currents of new life, largely American and Protestant in origin, which are running to-day in channels formed long ago by Spaniard and Catholic. Mexico was originally called "New Spain"; the character of its cities, its cathedrals, its language, and its art, might justify it in retaining this name. Here an ancient European civilization was transplanted to the home of an American civilization even more venerable, a civilization which has left records and

Photo by *Hugo Brehme, Mexico City.*

POPOCATEPETL, THE "SMOKING MOUNTAIN OF MEXICO"

"Here were the grandeur and beauty of Japan and Switzerland and California all in one place and at one time" (*p. 4*).

monuments as old, perhaps, as any known in Europe or in Asia. The atmosphere of age is over all — an air that I have not breathed since leaving China. The great cathedrals with their bells that clang by day and by night seem to set the approving seal of the Church upon the scene and to sound a warning against any attempts at transformation or change.

But signs of a different spirit are not lacking. Ford cars traverse the ancient streets; appeals for votes for this or that representative of the Republic adorn the monastery walls; the spire of a Protestant church rises in the very shadow of the great cathedral. Trenches, newly made and occupied in the last revolution, zigzag along the hill crest on which stands the bishop's palace built nearly three hundred years ago. They are a symbol of the violent reaction of the people against unfair and unscrupulous privilege and power, whether military or ecclesiastical.

The contrast between the everyday scenes in the United States and in Mexico has been well drawn by Señora Calderón de la Barca, wife of the first Spanish minister to Mexico, in her book, *Life in Mexico,* first published in 1842. Although her words were written eighty years ago, they are still apropos to-day:

"If anyone wishes to try the effect of a strong contrast, let him come direct from the United States to this country. It is in the villages especially that the contrast is most striking. Traveling in New England, for example, we arrive at a small and flourishing village. The wooden churches or meetinghouses are all new, all painted white, or perhaps a bright red. Hard by is a tavern with a green paling, as clean and as new as the churches, and there are also various smart stores and neat dwelling houses; all new, all wooden, all clean, and all ornamented with slight Grecian pillars. The whole has a cheerful, trim, and flourishing aspect. Houses, churches, stores, and taverns, all are of a piece. They are suited to the present emergency, whatever that may be, though they will never make fine ruins. Everything proclaims prosperity, equality, consistency; the past forgotten, the present all in all, and the future taking care of itself. No delicate attentions to posterity, who can never pay its debts. No beggars. If a man has even a hole in his coat, he must be lately from the Emerald Isle. . . .

"Transport yourself in imagination from this New England village to that of ——, it matters not which, not far from Mexico City. Look on this picture, and on that. At a little distance a hacienda, like a deserted palace, built of solid masonry, with its inner *patio* surrounded by thick stone pillars, with great walls and iron-barred windows that might stand a siege. Here a ruined arch and cross, so solidly built that one cannot but wonder how the stone ever crumbled away. There, rising in the midst of old, faithful-looking trees, the church, gray and ancient, but strong as if designed for eternity, with its saints and virgins, and martyrs and relics, its gold and silver and precious stones, whose value would buy up all the spare lots in the New England village; the leper with scarcely a rag to cover him, kneeling on the marble pavement.

"Here, everything reminds us of the past; of the conquering Spaniards, who seemed to build for eternity; impressing each work with their own solid, grave, and religious character; of the triumphs of Catholicism; and of the Indians when Cortes first startled them from their repose, and stood before them like the fulfillment of a half-forgotten prophecy. It is the present that seems like a dream, a pale reflection of the past. All is decaying and growing fainter, and men seem trusting to some unknown future which they may never see. One government has been abandoned, and there is none in its place. One revolution follows another, yet the remedy is not found. Let them beware lest half a century later, they be awakened from their delusion, and find the cathedral turned into a meetinghouse, and all painted white; the railing melted down; the silver transformed into dollars; the Virgin's jewels sold to the highest bidder; the floor washed (which would do it no harm), and round the whole, a nice new wooden paling, freshly done in green — and all this performed by some of the artists from the wide-awake republic farther north."

Señora Calderón de la Barca wrote these paragraphs thirty years before the entrance of the Protestant Church into Mexico. During these past twelve days we have seen something of the fruits of this movement. There may have been some loss in artistic values but there has been undeniable gain in character, in unselfish and practical service, in appreciation of truth and of brotherhood, and in true sonship with God through Christ.

At Monterey we were met by Dr. William Wallace, one of the veteran members of our Mission, and by two Mexican pastors. After reaching our hotel and before setting out on our work in that city, we paused for a brief prayer together. Dr. Rodgers prayed in Spanish and Señor Reynaldo Avila in English. Our hearts were united in these prayers; we thanked God for bringing us together; for the opportunity He had given us of serving Him in this land, and for the fellowship, both human and divine, in this service; and we prayed for His blessing upon the work of His Church both in Mexico and in the United States.

CHAPTER II

A SELF–SUPPORTING PROTESTANT CHURCH IN NORTHERN MEXICO

OAXACA, MEXICO,
November 4, 1922

THE six days from October 20 to 26 we spent in visiting the Presbyterian centers of work in five main cities situated on the table-land between the United States border and Mexico City.

The Presbyterian churches in these cities are all self-supporting and independent of the Mission and the Board, as far as current subsidies or formal relationships are concerned. They have become independent during the past three years, since the putting into effect of a division of territory and responsibility among the various Mission Boards at work in Mexico. A brief review of this co-operative plan of work is perhaps necessary to enable you to understand clearly the development of these Presbyterian churches.

The territorial division in Mexico among the various Missions was decided upon in 1914 when, at the taking of Vera Cruz by the United States marines in April of that year, all Americans were withdrawn from Mexico. There had been much overlapping and duplication of effort among the various denominations. Two thirds of the country was

fairly well served by Protestant forces, one third
of the territory had practically no resident missionaries. The evacuation of the country gave an
opportunity for readjustment and regrouping; the
initial plans for this step were laid at Cincinnati
in 1914; in Mexico City in 1917 and 1919, various
modifications were approved, but the general plan
stood as first proposed.

The work of our Mission had been chiefly in the
territory north of Mexico City. The Mission had
centers also in and near Mexico City and in the
state of Vera Cruz, and had a " sphere of interest "
in the six states and territories farther south.

This region was difficult to serve on account of
its climate and inaccessibility and, from a Protestant viewpoint, was the least developed in all Mexico. In 1914 our Mission and Board agreed to
withdraw from the cities north of Mexico City,
where other denominations were to work, and to
concentrate on meeting the needs in the southern
section, the Mission retaining a share of the work
in Mexico City and the Federal District.[1]

When the Cincinnati Plan was first proposed, it
was expected that the various native churches would
combine or affiliate with the denominational group
assigned to their respective cities. This combination took place in many instances, but in certain
cities the churches did not wish to change their denomination, and chose rather to continue independently without Mission subsidy. The Presbyterian churches in the five cities we visited all took

[1] For a more detailed description of the Cincinnati Plan and
coöperative developments, see Chapters XIV and XV.

this position; they helped to organize a " Presbytery of the National Frontier," and have gradually built up a self-supporting, self-propagating, and self-governing body. Their membership is now over 4,000, with twenty-seven individual churches; they contributed last year over 50,000 pesos, or more than $25,000 in American currency, out of a total of 80,000 pesos given by the Mexican Presbyterian Church as a whole. One church of 250 members gave 18,000 pesos last year; one of 200 members, 10,000 pesos, an average per member of fifty pesos or twenty-five dollars in American money. When you consider the average income of these people, you admire their spirit of sacrifice and devotion. There are not many Presbyterian churches in the United States that give in such proportion.

Our schedule called for travel by rail by day and for meetings and conferences in the afternoon and evening, with one-night stop-overs in each of the five cities. At Monterey, an iron and coal center of 85,000 people, we were met by two Mexican pastors, Reynaldo Avila and Pedro Rodríguez. The Presbyterian church was packed that night, and it was a joy to look into the faces of the people, to hear them sing the familiar hymns, and, in the service and the individual greetings after the meeting, to feel the bond of unity and fellowship that united us all. At Saltillo, a city of 35,000, known as the educational center of northern Mexico, we visited the fine, new building of the Girls' School, maintained by the Methodists, who have invested

$150,000 in this plant. We viewed the cathedrals of the city, also, with their great towers and massive walls and decorated interiors. The Protestant churches, Baptist and Presbyterian, that stood near by, seemed small and plain by comparison. Our church was little more than a roughly built hall, with whitewashed walls and ceiling. There was both pathos and truth in the Spanish inscription above the simple pulpit: " Surely God Is in This Place."

At San Luis Potosí, a city of 90,000, at an altitude of over 6,000 feet above sea level, and at Aguascalientes, with a growing population that now totals 65,000 people, a city famous for its hot springs and mineral waters, our native churches have just attained self-support. The Disciples Board (Christian Missionary Society) has missionaries in both these cities; they have been most generous and helpful in all their relations with our churches and with our Mission's representatives. At Aguascalientes the whole native Protestant community was represented, and after the meeting we had an informal conference with the leaders of the three denominations at work there. At Saltillo the Presbyterian pastor is Leandro Garza Mora; at San Luis Potosí, Pedro Garcia; at Aguascalientes, Pablo Mena y Jiménez; at Zacatecas, Pedro Rameres.

The service in Zacatecas was held under the most unusual circumstances of any of the meetings which we attended. This town is 8,010 feet above sea level. It was formerly a center for silver mines

CHURCH AND GIANT CYPRESS IN OAXACA

"There, rising in the midst of old faithful-looking trees, the church, gray and ancient, but strong as if designed for eternity" (p. 6).

of great value and in 1910 had a population of about 80,000 people. The mines were abandoned during the series of revolutions which spanned the years 1910–1920, and the population has dwindled to a scant 12,000. Everywhere were deserted adobe houses, crumbling arches and walls, and over all a general air of ruin and desolation. It seemed a city of the dead; and the white sanctuary at the crest of the mountain back of the city, with the inscription, "Viva Maria," in black letters across its walls, seemed its tombstone.

Our Mission owns a vast edifice which was formerly the chapel of the Convent of Saint Augustine; it had been confiscated by the government during one of the earlier revolutions, and later the Mission had purchased it at a low cost. We entered the chapel through a subterranean passage like the corridor of a feudal castle. When we emerged, the light from the white walls and ceiling was almost dazzling. The walls were fully fifty feet in height; above the center of the church rose a dome, the ceiling of which was eighty feet above the floor. The niches in the walls where the images of the saints had stood had been filled up; in their places were New Testament texts in gilt letters. That night services were held in this church; the great dome above us which had once resounded with the chant of friar and nun gave back to us the echoes of our Protestant hymns; and as I listened to the pastor tell of the battle the Protestant Church was waging in Mexico and of the persecution it was enduring, and as I looked about at the transformed interior of this venerable ecclesiastical building, it seemed that the clock of time had slipped back, that we had been translated to the early sixteenth century, and that we were now witnesses of the launching of the Reformation.

The next day, the twenty-sixth, we left Zacatecas for Mexico City. The days had been tremendously full. Our minds were flooded with new impressions and experiences. But more real and lasting than any memories of strange and novel scenes, or of a people invariably picturesque, were the impressions in our hearts of the courage of our Mexican brothers, of their spirit of sacrifice on behalf of the Church, and of our deep and true fellowship in Christ.

CHAPTER III

THE MISSIONARY MESSAGE IN THE MOUNTAINS OF OAXACA

Oaxaca, Mexico,
November 8, 1922

ON Tuesday, October 31, we left Mexico City *en route* for Oaxaca (pronounced Wa-ha-ka), the youngest station in our Mexico Mission. We spent a day and a half in Puebla, a strong center of Methodist work, on our way to Oaxaca, and had five days in and near Oaxaca City. I am writing you now concerning our experiences there.

The state of Oaxaca has a population of 1,000,000 people and an area of about 35,000 square miles, roughly that of Indiana. There are few large cities in the state, Oaxaca City, the capital, having 40,000 people, and the next largest city, Zaachila, having a population of 13,000. Innumerable small towns and villages are scattered among the mountains and practically every trail leads to one of these little clusters of thatched adobe houses. Eighty per cent of the people in the city and ninety-five per cent of those in the country are pure-blooded Indians, chiefly of the Mixtecan and Zapotecan races. Porfirio Diaz and Benito Juárez were natives of Oaxaca, and there is a strong spirit of local pride and independence among its citizens.

Our Board and Church are the only ones at work in the state and have the full responsibility for carrying the Protestant message to the people there. Our missionary force consists of two couples, Rev. and Mrs. L. P. Van Slyke, and Rev. and Mrs. A. W. Wolfe. Mr. and Mrs. Wolfe have been in Mexico for three years, but have been in Oaxaca only ten months; Mr and Mrs. Van Slyke have been in the state for two years. Both couples are stationed in Oaxaca City, though their work radiates far to the east and to the west.

Oaxaca City is a twelve-hour ride on a narrow-gauge railroad from Puebla. The mountain ranges which we saw from the train were far rougher and more irregular than those on the plateau to the north. *Organo* cactus, with clustered stems like the pipes of an organ, grew in profusion on the mountain sides. We crossed various streams, and it was good to see running water after the arid stretches of the table-land. The valleys in Oaxaca are most fertile, and we saw evidences of their productivity in the sugar cane, corn, alfalfa, grapefruit, oranges, and bananas which grew along the railway. The track was only three feet in width and the grades were exceptionally steep, being over three per cent in certain sections.

Oaxaca is a great mining center, but the revolutions have driven away most of the foreign capitalists. The American population of Oaxaca City before the revolution was over two hundred; now

there are less than twenty, mostly miners and pros-
pectors, with only one household in addition to our
two missionary families.

On the train there was the usual military guard,
the soldiers riding on top of the box cars which were
in front of the passenger coaches. We reached
Oaxaca City Friday night and learned later that
the next train which ran from Puebla to Oaxaca
on Saturday was attacked by a group of bandits
and revolutionaries, with the express car as their
objective. Two soldiers were killed and, according
to the report which the American consul gave us
here, two Mexican passengers were killed and two
were wounded. The guard drove off the attackers,
and the train came through, although it was late in
reaching the city. Such occurrences, however, are
rare and we do not expect to come so near one
again.

We had started at five o'clock in the morning
and we reached Oaxaca City about six in the evening. We were met at the station by the Van
Slykes and the Wolfes. It was growing dark as
we drove home with them. All about us lay the
strange city, with its multitude of unfamiliar sights
and sounds. For the first time since we had reached
Mexico, we had the sensation of isolation in a foreign land. Here were no Americans except these
two young couples; nothing to recall the familiar
scenes and activities of the homeland. The stars
shone over the silent hills beyond the city borders,
and America seemed far away. With a rush the
memories of my own first experiences on the mis-

sion field came flooding back; the sense of isolation, the wave of loneliness, and the feeling that only the power and presence of God could steady and keep one happy and strong in the work. It seemed as if one ought to reach out and touch Him to fortify oneself for what was ahead by this living and tangible contact. Surely the men and women who give up their homeland and all that is dear in it to work in such alien centers deserve the hundredfold blessing that Christ has promised to those who will relinquish loved possessions for His sake. Surely Christ's Church in the United States should see that these men and women are given the moral and financial support which will enable them to do an effective and lasting work for Him.

During our stay in Oaxaca, we have seen and met with congregations both in the city and in the mountainous country outside. On Sunday morning, the fifth, we went to the church and Sunday school, where Mr. Day spoke, and where we heard a young Indian, named Martin Lopez, tell of his narrow escape at the hands of a Catholic mob which attacked him and two other young Protestants who had been preaching in a near-by village. His head was still bandaged, and the simple story which he told recalled vividly the persecutions suffered by the early apostles and by the Protestant leaders of the Reformation. We had seen one of his companions, Alfonso Sosa, in the hospital at Puebla, and had heard his account of the attack there. In another letter I want to tell you the story of the two men as they told it to us.

Sunday evening we met in the church again and Dr. Rodgers and I spoke, telling of the prayers and good wishes of the Presbyterian Church in the United States expressed in a letter which the Moderator of the General Assembly, Dr. C. C. Hays, had given us to transmit to the Presbyterian churches in this country. The meeting was held in a church building which our Mission had purchased from the Methodists, following the transfer of territory between their Mission and ours. The building is in an excellent location, but half of it is unroofed and has never been completed, so that the general effect is not happy. The church property contains rooms which might be of service for institutional work; there is room for expansion, but it will require $10,000 to complete the present auditorium and to put the building into a presentable condition. This is the only Protestant church in the city and the only one of its size in the whole state. The local congregation has made, and is making, a sacrificial contribution to the completion of the church. Surely there must be individuals in the United States who will see the strategic importance of supplying the necessary additional equipment for the work which this group of Christ's followers can do in the capital city of a great state.

Monday and Tuesday, the sixth and the seventh, we spent in visiting two congregations in the country; one of them at Rancho del Águila, the other at a little town called Nazareno. The first was reached after a half hour's ride on the narrow-gauge train, and a seven hour's horseback ride

across the plain and over a mountain range. Mr.
Wolfe and Mr. Van Slyke accompanied us, as did
also a Mexican evangelist called Marciano Cruz.
Our blankets and extra outfit were packed on three
burros, and we made quite a cavalcade as we moved
off. It was a joy to be in the saddle, riding under
the blue sky toward the mountains which stood out
in such crisp outline in the clear Mexican air. The
trail over the mountains carried us up over 3,000
feet so that we were over 9,000 feet above sea level
when we reached the top.

The service at Aguila was held in a little church
built of roughhewn boards and shingles. The
houses that clustered near looked much like the
thatched houses in a mountain hamlet in Switzerland, and the sound of a horn blown to call the people to the services added to the Swiss atmosphere.
The people who came into the little church were all
Mixtecan Indians, the women wrapped in *rebozos*
(shawls), many of them carrying babies, and the
men in serapes and broad-brimmed sombreros.
Most of them did not understand Spanish and it
was necessary for Mr. Day and me to speak first
in English, which Mr. Van Slyke translated into
Spanish, his words again being put into Mixtecan
by one of the Indians. The candles and the lamp
in the little church shone dimly and at times flick-
ered and almost went out. So, it seemed to us,
the light of the gospel had burned in this mountain
village, feeble but kept aglow as a witness to the
fidelity of the missionary and the evangelist, and as
a promise of the brighter day to come.

Some of us slept that night on the wooden platform of the church as there was no room elsewhere, and early next morning we started for the trip down the mountain to Nazareno. There in a room of one of the adobe houses the second service was held, with Indians in attendance as at Aguila. There is a remarkable beauty and nobility of expression in the faces of some of these Indians that justifies the description of Señora Calderón de la Barca quoted in an earlier letter. Jesus was known as the Nazarene and our hope and prayer is that many of these people may be led to follow in his steps.

Aguila and Nazareno are only two points in one of the circuits which Mr. Van Slyke regularly covers. His full schedule on this mountain route on horseback runs like this:

"Etna (by rail) to Nazareno, 1 hour
Nazareno to Aguila, 7 hours
To Oro, 1½ hours
To Santa Inez, 3 hours
To Nuxaa, 3 hours
To Carizal, 3 hours
To Rio Minas, 3 hours
To San Francisco de Telixtlahuaca, 5 hours
To Nazareno again, 3 hours."

All this over mountain ranges and valleys by a rough, broken trail with another circuit on the other side of the railroad! Mr. Wolfe has an even more extensive route in another direction among the Zapotecs. But a whole section of the state to the south is not covered at all, and the city has openings on every hand.

Our work in Oaxaca is still in its pioneer stages. The gospel is being preached verbally; the comradeship and counsel of the pastor are being freely given; and the sacraments of the Church are being administered. But there is need for the development of our full fourfold program of service in evangelism, education, medicine, and the supplying of Christian literature. The first steps in educational work have been taken by Mr. and Mrs. Van Slyke in providing room and board in their own house for a dozen boys and girls attending city schools, and by Mr. and Mrs. Wolfe in purchasing a lot in Telixtlahuaca for the site of a "work-your-way" school for the poorer boys. These two young missionaries and their wives, with the local church leaders, are making a brave endeavor to meet the needs of the field. But they cannot do it without reënforcements. The Station is asking for an additional ordained missionary, for a doctor, and for a woman missionary for social service. The field is there, the need is there, the setting is fascinating, the call is clear and strong. "He that hath ears to hear, let him hear."

NATIVE CART IN OAXACA

The Roman yoke, resembling the yokes employed in Palestine in the time of Christ, is used in Latin-American countries.

CHAPTER IV

THE COST OF DISCIPLESHIP IN MEXICO TO-DAY

En Route to ORIZABA,
November 10, 1922

IN Mexico the observer of religious conditions feels as if he were living in the early days of the Reformation.

The Roman Catholic Church is visible everywhere, the Catholic Church as it was prior to the Reformation and not as we know it in the United States. The Protestant movement in Mexico is just beginning to gather strength. One of the tragic consequences of the interaction of these two religious bodies is the occasional but too frequent persecutions of the Protestants by the Catholics. Despite the generally observed constitutional article guaranteeing freedom of religious belief, these attacks are sometimes made with much of the fierceness and unrestraint of the persecutions of the so-called heretics of the early sixteenth century.

From reports we received as we traveled through the country, there appears to have been a recrudescence of such attacks in the past few months. These reports come from all sections of the country; from Durango in the north, from Chiapas in the south, and from the central states. Concerning some of these attacks we have received accounts at first hand: I will give the story of two of them as they were told to us.

The first attack was upon a young Protestant lad in Matehuala, in the state of San Luis Potosí, north of Mexico City. The incident occurred about four months ago. The boy was a native of that town and was a member of the Friends Church. The priest of the Roman Catholic Church there had preached a violent sermon, inciting the congregation to attack all Protestants, declaring that it was a religious duty to kill them. This Protestant boy was passing the church when the service ended; the people came rushing out and fell upon him. He was knocked down, beaten, and left for dead. His old mother, hearing of the attack, came up sometime later, found that he was still living and had regained consciousness, and tried to pick him up to carry him away. She succeeded in dragging him about three hundred yards toward their home. The Catholic crowd again collected and, seeing the boy's condition, told him that if he would call out, "*Viva la Virgin de Guadalupe!*" they would let him live. He replied, "I can never do that; I know in Whom I have believed," whereupon the mob closed in upon him and killed him.

This account was given us by Rev. J. P. Hauser of the Methodist Mission at Puebla, on November 2.

The account of the second attack we took down ourselves from the lips of two young Protestants who had narrowly escaped death. One of them was named Alfonso Sosa, the other, Martin Lopez.

Both were members of the Presbyterian Church
in the state of Oaxaca from which we have just
come. This attack occurred on September 6, 1922,
in the little village of Yucanama near Teposcolula,
in the northwestern part of the state. Sosa is about
twenty-five years old; Lopez is somewhat younger.
Sosa has been a teacher in government schools;
last year he taught in the Presbyterian school in
Huaclilla. He was also for a short time a student
in the theological seminary in Mexico City. We
saw him in the Latin American Hospital maintained by the Baptists and Methodists at Puebla.
Lopez we heard speak in the Presbyterian church
in Oaxaca City. Both were still bandaged. According to the report given us by Dr. Wall in the
Puebla hospital, Sosa had sustained a cut from a
machete which went to the bone from ear to nose
on his right cheek, his right arm was broken, the
third finger on his left hand was shot away, and his
head and body were severely cut and bruised.
Lopez's skull was fractured, his left arm was
broken, and he was also cut and bruised. Their
wounds were seriously infected, due to the four-
days' delay in proper treatment.

Sosa's story, as he told it to us in the hospital
and as it was translated from Spanish into English,
was as follows:

"Rev. A. W. Wolfe, of the Presbyterian Mission
at Oaxaca, Martin Lopez, and I were on an itiner-
ating tour in northern Oaxaca. We had been
threatened in Yucanama, a town of about four
hundred people, some weeks before, and we had

therefore secured a safe conduct from the governor of the state. We had not expected to go to Yucanama again on this trip, but the group of believers there, about ten in number, asked us to come and hold service. Mr. Wolfe had gone on to Teposcolula; but Lopez and I went to Yucanama and held a service there that night. Next morning the owner of the house was put in jail on the ground that his house door was open after eight o'clock, a local law requiring that all houses be closed at that hour. I asked permission to visit him in jail, but this was denied me.

" We left town about nine-thirty, September 6, to go to Teposcolula, four and a half miles away, where Mr. Wolfe had gone. A believer from Yucanama accompanied us. As we reached the edge of the town we saw people gathering. We had gone about a quarter of a mile when they began to cross the road in front of us and to threaten us. After another quarter of a mile we approached a little ravine. The people were insulting us and I was afraid we would be attacked in the ravine, so we turned back toward town. Then they surrounded us and began to stone us. I talked to them trying to persuade them to stop; then I was hit with a large stone in the body, and a man came close with a pointed revolver. I put up my left hand and the bullet went through my hand, smashing one of my fingers. Then we ran into the field; Lopez was knocked down with stones; the brother from Yucanama was hit with stones, but he got away and Lopez also escaped.

" The crowd kept stoning me and shooting at me. One of them hit me across the face with a machete; when I fell I lifted up my right arm to protect myself and it was broken by a blow from a machete: I heard other pistol shots; then I fainted.

" When I waked up after two hours a man who was passing by called out, ' Are you not dead yet? ' and then went on. I asked him to carry me away but he refused. About seven in the evening I dragged myself away through the fields. Soon I saw some people coming up in the moonlight with stones and rifles. They came to me and carried me up into the hills. I asked for water and then I asked them to allow me to make a prayer. I prayed for myself and for them and I told them that if they would pick up the books and Bibles which had been thrown out along the roadside, they would find things good for them; I tried to preach the gospel to them.

" They took me to the top of the hill and said, ' You are in bad shape, we had better put you out of your misery.' ' No,' I said, ' leave me here; God will take care of me.' So they left me.

" I stayed there all night. Next morning I felt better; the bleeding had stopped and I found that I could get up and could walk. I walked over the hills toward a town called San Juan Topostoluca. When I saw some men looking for me I hid from them and about ten o'clock reached the town. Some believers lived there and they made a litter and carried me to Teposcolula where Mr. Wolfe was. We reached there at 1.30 P.M. September 7.

"That night we stayed there. The next evening Mr. Wolfe and ten others started carrying Lopez and me to the railroad at Parian, forty miles away. We arrived there the evening of the ninth and reached Puebla the evening of the tenth."

Sosa told his story simply, without raising his voice and with no visible malice toward his persecutors.

Four days later, in the Presbyterian church in Oaxaca, we heard Lopez speak of the same incident. He said that when he was knocked down, he called out, "O Jesus, save me!" One of the villagers seemed to take pity on him and helped him up, and so he escaped to the hills and then to Teposcolula where there were friends.

Long after Lopez ceased speaking his words echoed in our ears, "O Jesus, save me!" That prayer of a humble follower of Christ in desperate need was answered. There is need to-day for prayers of equal sincerity that Jesus will save His Church in Mexico from hatred and violence and from all that is contrary to His will of peace and truth and love.

Rev. A. W. Wolfe has reported the death of three Protestant workers in January, 1923, in this same district. He wrote:

"Some months later, a brother who closely resembles Alfonso Sosa, visited Teposcolula, and the report that Alfonso had returned without a scar scared some of the Indians nearly to death. That was their only punishment, as Señor Calles took no notice of complaints lodged with him.

" The following January the same priest and the same politician who incited and protected the assassins of Yucanama stirred up trouble in San Juan Teposcolula where thirty families were worshiping under the sincere but indiscreet leadership of Feliciano Martinez, a lad just over twenty-one, of promising intelligence and great consecration. Following a rousing sermon by the priest, sixty armed men took Feliciano from his home at night, hacked him to pieces, and carried his head and his heart as an offering to the image of Mary in their church. A devoted friend, Fernando Reyes, died with him. Another was killed later. All the Protestants were compelled to flee or recant; and all the families but one fled, losing most of their property.

" No one was ever punished; but one of the murderers became a captain in the army of De la Huerta. Our workers have not ceased to visit the Mixteca. The blood of martyrs has bought it for Christ. Probably Rome will take more lives before religious toleration and an open Bible become the rule in these mountains; but we go forward.

' It is the way the Master went;
  Should not the servant tread it still? ' "

CHAPTER V

THE THREEFOLD SERVICE OF THE CHURCH IN ORIZABA

En Route to Vera Cruz,
November 11, 1922

AT five-thirty on the morning of November 9 we left Oaxaca for Puebla, *en route* to Orizaba. The passenger coach in which we rode was marked by bullets which had been fired in a raid on the train made five days before.

We learned at Puebla that the attacking party thought some high military official was on the train and therefore opened fire on the first-class coach as well as on the military guard farther forward. The revised list of casualties showed three soldiers killed and seven wounded, one train employee killed, one first-class passenger killed and several wounded. The last car of our train on the ninth was the pay car of the road, and some of the more nervous passengers grew apprehensive when, about three o'clock in the afternoon, the train stopped in the center of a wide plain. The engine was detached and off it went, ostensibly for some needed repairs, leaving us engineless in the middle of a cornfield on the plain. It was dark before another engine returned but we reached Puebla without a mishap about eleven o'clock that evening.

The next morning we left for Orizaba. Puebla is 7,200 feet above sea level. Orizaba is a little over 4,000 feet in altitude. The route between the two cities is most picturesque, and reminds one of certain portions of the Canadian Pacific line. The drop of 3,000 feet between the two cities is largely made in one section of seventeen miles, between Galera and Maltrata. The view of the latter village, as we saw it shining in the sunlight below us from our vantage point on the cloud-wrapped mountains above, was beautiful and impressive. Above us towered Mt. Orizaba, the second highest peak on the North American continent and the third highest in the Western Hemisphere. That day, however, the clouds hid it from our sight.

Orizaba is a city of about 35,000 inhabitants, situated half-way between the *tierra caliente* (hot country) of the coast and the highlands of the central plateau. It is a center for cotton mills, sugar, and coffee; ordinarily, business there is most prosperous, but now, like most of the cities we have visited, it is experiencing a depression due to the effects of the revolutions in the past and to the uncertainty of guarantees as to the future.

Our Mission and Vera Cruz Station are represented by Rev. and Mrs. Newell J. Elliott. Aside from a single family representing the Plymouth Brethren, there are no other missionaries in the city, and the main responsibility for Protestant work there rests upon our own Church. We have two main properties, which we acquired by purchase from the Methodists after they had evacuated the district and city in accordance with the Cincinnati Plan. One of these properties, on Escandon Street, includes the church building and also the residence of the pastor, Placido Lope, and several rooms which are used as a dispensary. The latter represents an interesting experiment in medical service. Dr. M. P. Colmenares, a physician of good reputation in the city, offers his services without charge in the direction of this dispensary, and Mr. and Mrs. Elliott assist in its administration. Only people who do not have the money to buy drugs, or who are in evident need, are served by the dispensary. It was opened in August, 1921, and since January 1, 1922, 577 prescriptions for people of this type have been filled and four major operations have been performed in the little operating room.

In the other property, on Calle Reforma, are located a school for boys and girls and the residence of Mr. and Mrs. Elliott. In the school, which is of primary grade, including the first six years of instruction according to the governmental standards, are enrolled 123 students, evenly divided between boys and girls. The principal of this school is a Mexican lady, Señora Sherwell, who is most efficient. There are three other Mexican teachers but no " foreigners " on the faculty. The school is administered at a small expense and is undoubtedly meeting a vital need in the community.

On the evening of November 10, the day of our arrival at Orizaba, the closing exercises of the school were held in the Llave Theater. Practically all the seats and boxes in the theater were taken and the audience was cordial and appreciative. Songs were sung and games were played by little children of the kindergarten, who made a most happy and appealing impression. Little Red Riding Hood, *La Capercita,* was acted by the children of the lower primary grades. The childish voices, with their sweet Spanish cadences, sounded clearly through the theater and surely reached the hearts of some of those who had come in a spirit of indifference or of open antagonism to all for which the school stood. Diplomas were given out to the graduating students and the performance, in true Latin-American style, continued until after midnight.

The next day we visited the various properties, conferred with the local pastor, with Mr. and Mrs. Elliott, and with two Mexican leaders who had come from Vera Cruz to meet us. At three o'clock we started on the four-hour trip by rail which would bring us to Vera Cruz.

The work at Orizaba has passed the stage of oral exhortation and already there are visible developments along educational and medical lines. These developments are good and are clearly worth while. But in these three types of service for body, mind, and spirit, there is need for greater integration and cohesion, and the pervading consciousness that, in Christ, they are not three but one.

CHAPTER VI

VERA CRUZ, THE CITY OF THE TRUE CROSS

En Route to Chiapas,
November 15, 1922

ON November 11 we left Orizaba by rail and in four hours dropped down 4,000 feet to the sea level at Vera Cruz.

There is a spirit and atmosphere about any city or locality where events of historical importance have taken place, or where human attention has been repeatedly centered, that is more than subjectively pervasive and real. Such an atmosphere perceptibly exists in Vera Cruz. To one without a knowledge of Mexican history, it would at once be apparent: when one remembers the events that have taken place there during the past four centuries, there is ample justification for such an historical aura.

Into Vera Cruz Harbor on April 21, 1519, rode the ships of Hernando Cortes, the first European to visit its shores; there these ships were sunk that his men might have no retreat; from Vera Cruz he set out on the expedition that was to result in the downfall of the Aztec Empire under the Montezumas, the acquisition by the Spanish sovereign of "New Spain" and eventually of territory ranging from the sources of the

34

THE MOONLIT BAY OF VERA CRUZ

In the distance the Castle of San Juan de Ulua, "over which last floated the Spanish flag in Mexico" (*p. 35*).

Mississippi River to Cape Horn, one half of the total territory of the three Americas. Over the castle of San Juan de Ulúa last floated the Spanish flag, before it was finally furled in 1824, when Mexico became a free and independent state. In 1847, American warships gathered in the bay, and an American army invaded the city; in 1862, a fleet of French, Spanish, and English vessels anchored there as a prelude to the enactment of the drama that was to place a Hapsburg prince on an American throne; on April 21, 1914, on the same day of the month that Cortes landed there, but five years less than four centuries later, American cruisers entered the bay and United States marines took possession of the city. So the turbulent drama of Mexican history, its glory and its pathos, have been epitomized in the pageantry of this port.

The responsibility for the development of the Protestant movement in this important city was transferred to our Mission and Board, following the approval of the Cincinnati Plan. Our work is being developed in four distinct ways. Señor Rosales is pastor of the local church. There on Sunday, Mr. Day spoke in the morning and Dr. Rodgers and I in the evening. Señor Rosales was formerly a Methodist, as that denomination was at work in Vera Cruz before 1914; he is now working with our Presbyterians in the true spirit of co-operation which the Cincinnati Plan aimed to foster and build up. Medical work is represented by a free dispensary for the poor, the forerunner of the dispensary in Orizaba which we had already visited.

A local Mexican doctor is giving his time freely to the service there; Señor Mirabal Lausan manages the detailed work of the dispensary and the reading room associated with it, with Mr. Elliott as general supervisor.

A little monthly magazine called *El Faro* — The Lighthouse — is published in the office of the dispensary. This magazine supplements the larger union magazine called *El Mundo Cristiano* which is the organ of all the Protestant Churches in Mexico. Quotations from *El Faro* have been made in the publications of such far-away cities as Quezaltenango, Guatemala, and Lima, Peru; the rays of this little lighthouse thus radiate from Mexico to Central and South America.

Educationally, there is a primary school in the city under the management of Señorita Rioja, which receives purely local support. In a fine location near the beach and the new lighthouse of the port, there is a primary and secondary school for girls administered by our Mission. Miss Mary F. Turner is the *directora*. Miss M. B. Taylor and temporarily Miss Ethel Doctor are teachers there. The school, which is called *Instituto Morelos,* is a successor of the former school under the principalship of Miss Turner in Aguascalientes, which was given up in accordance with the Cincinnati Plan, in 1916. The present enrollment is eighty-five. The school is in rented quarters, although rents in Vera Cruz are abnormally high. Our Mission and Board maintain two other schools for girls in Mexico, one of which still lacks permanent property, as in Vera Cruz, and it has been a strain upon the current budget of the Mission to continue the payments for rent and upkeep necessary for the maintenance of these three schools. The problem would be largely solved if funds for property could be secured.

On November 14, we left Vera Cruz for the three-day journey which will take us to Chiapas. On the train we talked with an oil prospector, who, on behalf of a New York corporation, is drilling a new well near Vera Cruz. He said that already over $200,000 had been spent in sinking this single well, with no return as yet. I thought of what could be accomplished by the investment of such a sum in the work which our missionaries are carrying on in Mexico; how it would meet our need for property for our institutions, and of the visible returns which we had seen obtained through the investment of a mere fraction of such a sum.

Our work goes forward through increased financial support but the true secret of that portion of it which is living and which will be permanent, rests not on money for the work but on the sacrificial spirit of the workers. The road to new life and to salvation from the many ills to which Mexico is heir is by this sacrificial way; in this way the representatives of our Church, who are so bravely contending against heavy odds in Vera Cruz, have a unique opportunity and responsibility to make the city in fact as well as in name, the place of the True Cross.

CHAPTER VII

SOME IMPRESSIONS OF THE PRESENT POLITICAL AND ECONOMIC SITUATION IN MEXICO

November 20, 1924

WE have been one month in the Republic of Mexico and many impressions have been formed in our minds, so varied that it is a matter of extreme difficulty to set them down in any logical order. Our study before coming prepared us to survey a very old civilization. We had learned that its roots run back into a dim antiquity. This civilization had had imposed upon it three hundred years of unrestricted and ruthless Spanish rule. In 1810 the people of Mexico began a revolution which was destined to end in the independence of the country in 1824. Since that date its rulers have been from among Mexico's own people (with the exception of the short sway of Maximilian, who was foisted upon the country by the French at the invitation of the Roman Catholic priests).

At the end of the autocratic rule of Porfirio Diaz there started in Mexico what is now called the "Revolution," which lasted for eleven years during which some ten different men held the reins of power, the chief figures being Madero, De la Huerta, Carranza, and the present President Obregon who has held office for about two years. During Carranza's administration a new Constitution for Mexico was drawn up based on the Constitution promulgated on February 5, 1857, under Benito Juárez. The Carranza Government adopted this new Constitution also on February 5 in the year 1917. It is because of provisions in this latter Constitution affecting the ownership of property in Mexico by foreigners that the government of President Obregon has not been recognized by the United States of America. This Constitution forbids the ownership of any real estate by a religious body or its representatives, and with relation to all other foreign owners of property, clauses in the Constitution have been interpreted as forbidding ownership unless the foreign owner will place himself entirely under Mexican laws as a Mexican with regard to such property. The "nationalization" of minerals and of products of the subsoil, including oil, and the question as to whether these provisions are retroactive have been given much attention in our American press.

The Constitution also provides that large estates may be taken over by the government and parceled out to small owners, compensation being made for properties thus taken. Many large estates have thus been broken up, in some cases without any compensation being made to prior owners, in other cases the government making payment in bonds which, it is claimed, are worthless. Not infrequently the main ranch house and some surrounding land has been left to the former owners, but in the state of Yucatan it has been common to take over the entire estate and to parcel it out, leaving nothing to the family who had inherited the property.

It ought to be said that it is the common understanding that most of these large estates had been acquired in various military campaigns or by other more or less ruthless methods. The lands have been taken from tribal or communal groups: these, of course, were really Indian tribes which from the earliest times have held large districts, each man cultivating whatever portion he desired. The large estates of modern times represent lands taken from entire tribes or communities, and the present " confiscation " is simply a method in the eyes of the people of returning the land to the former tribes or communities. To put it in plain language, it is returning stolen property to the rightful owners.

The present situation is one of rather unstable equilibrium, for although the process as described is going on with the sanction of the government, owners are living in hope that something will put an end to the system of confiscation and that they will be restored to their prior rights. Many fine pieces of property have been turned over by the government to generals of the successful revolutionary armies whose enjoyment of them depends entirely upon the maintenance of the present régime. To the credit of President Obregon be it said that he has compelled the restitution of a great deal of such property to owners who were despoiled by the revolutionaries. There are many complications and variations in the situation, but it can readily be seen that it is almost impossible to transfer any considerable property at the present time by ordinary sale and purchase, as all titles are practically in doubt, and prospective purchasers are very doubtful as to what they are actually getting when they pay the purchase price.

This is the basic cause of the slowing down of business which has been in evidence in the republic for some time, and which has been marked by a rather precipitous movement since October, 1921; the month of October, 1922, being the worst, from a business standpoint, during this period. To add to the business depression, crops have been short for three years in many of the states because of the lack of moisture. The masses of the people have nothing with which to trade at the shops in the cities and towns. This makes for general discontent and a great deal of the local banditry is due to these severe economic conditions. Not long ago it was reported by a villager in the mountains that a band from a neighboring village had attacked a train, " as they always do when they have a short crop." The vicious circle is complete: political instability and confiscatory laws render the position of capital and especially of real estate uncertain; current business is paralyzed; discontent is engendered and becomes bold; governmental authority is threatened and defied, making for political instability and revolution.

Two world movements are involved in these factors of the vicious circle and give impulse to them: one is the radical or communistic revolt against capitalism, and the other the depression in business which is general throughout the world. In the first mentioned of these Mexico has participated to a degree second only to Russia and the peak has not yet been reached. In Vera Cruz, Red demonstrations are an almost daily occurrence, and tenants who decide that they will no longer pay rent hang a red flag out of the window or over the front door to signify their repudiation of this contractual obligation. They continue to occupy the premises, and the United States consul in Vera Cruz told us that owners consider themselves helpless. In the state of Yucatan where formerly capital had become most despotic and ruthless the reaction is likewise most radical. Both the mayor of Vera Cruz and the governor of Yucatan are radical anti-capitalists.

The heaviest taxes levied against Mexicans fall upon the shopkeepers who are almost being ruined by this form of confiscation. Small manufacturers also feel the heavy weight of the tax burden almost to the point of annihilation. This may be either local or state taxation. One instance came directly under our eye at Oaxaca in which a soap manufacturer, thoroughly expert in the business, whose small but complete plant was located near the home of an American, was compelled to shut down because of the high local taxes imposed. He is able, however, to manufacture his product in the hills some fifteen miles from the city and to have it hauled to the town in oxcarts, thereby avoiding the municipal tax. A small dealer in cheap shoes told the writer that it was practically impossible for him to make any money owing to the fact that he was compelled to pay sixty pesos (thirty dollars) as a monthly tax.

The difficulties of employers of labor cannot be appreciated without some understanding of the attitude of labor and the leaders of labor unions in Mexico. In many localities they use the red and black banner, the radical emblem. In some instances they have taken complete possession of factories in which they were formerly employed, and are attempting to operate them by themselves. The shipping at the ports of Vera Cruz and Progreso is completely at the mercy of the unions, who fix the terms and hours of work according to their own ideas. We saw thousands of packages of paper, each package weighing not less than 250 pounds, dumped out on the ground near the docks in Vera Cruz last spring, by the unionized stevedores who have refused to move it since, owing to some difference between the union and the shipping companies. The rains of five months have of course ruined the paper.

President Obregon has thus far shown himself capable of holding matters with a firm and steady hand, having put down all local uprisings. In spite of an undercurrent of opposition the president has boldly taken steps to reduce the army, but every train has its quota of soldiers ready for defense in case of attacks from bandits or revolutionaries.

There are, however, other factors which must be mentioned as favorable. Mine owners are no longer robbed of their dynamite and then compelled to buy it back from the robbers, though mining operations have by no means been resumed on a large scale. Operators are enjoying a greater sense of security. The repair shops for the railway in Monterey and Aguascalientes are gradually increasing the number of men employed, and the smelter at Monterey has 1,500 men at work. Large grazing areas which had been denuded of cattle are being stocked again, the papers reporting that many thousands of head have been driven across the northern boundary line from Arizona and New Mexico. The magnificent grazing lands of Chiapas in the far south were made picturesque by the herds which we were told had wholly disappeared during the latter years of the revolution.

The testimony of business men residing in Mexico is quite contradictory as to the present state of business and its trend. Some men who have remained continuously in Mexico during the entire period of revolution and since, told us that conditions are better than they have been for fifteen years. On the other hand, we heard of man after man who had conducted successful business enterprises in Mexico for many years, who now has given up and left the country. Some advisers strongly urge that the wave of confiscation or "denouncement" of property has about subsided and that the present is the very time to make purchases of real estate, taking such title as can be acquired either by a civil incorporated company or by an individual. Schools and social centers can be established and

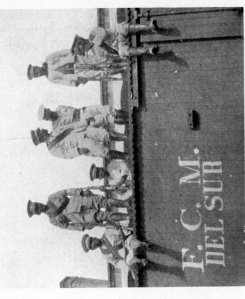

GUARD ON TRAIN TO CHIAPAS (*p. 46*).   SOLDIERS ON TRAIN TO OAXACA (*pp. 17, 30*).

RAILWAY TRANSPORTATION IN MEXICO

Despite these militaristic indications, life and property are as safe to-day in Mexico as in New York City.

assembly rooms provided in which church groups can meet without molestation, and without subjecting the property to denouncement on the ground that it belongs to a religious body. Certainly there are in a number of our Presbyterian centers attractive properties to be had at low prices.[1]

DWIGHT H. DAY

[1] For further discussion of these topics, see Chapters XVI to XVIII inclusive.

CHAPTER VIII

THE CHALLENGE OF THE CHURCH IN CHIAPAS

En Route to JALAPA,
November 23, 1922

THE work that is being done for Christ in the state of Chiapas holds a unique place in the forward movement of our Church in Mexico to-day.

This work is unique, first, because of its location. Chiapas is in the most inaccessible and the least developed portion of Mexico. The eastern boundary of the state is contiguous with the northern border of Guatemala; on the south lies the Pacific Ocean which we glimpsed from the train as we skirted its shores; on the north and west are the undeveloped states of Oaxaca and Tabasco. The trip by train from Vera Cruz to Tapachula, the chief center of our work in Chiapas, took us three days; Tuxtla Gutiérrez, the state capital, is three days by horseback from the nearest point on the railroad. The state has a population of approximately 400,000 and in area is about the size of the state of Ohio. Palenque, the ancient capital of the Itzas, whose walls were built nearly two thousand years before Christ, is in Chiapas; over eighty per cent of the inhabitants of the state to-day are pure-blooded Indians. Some of these Indians are descendants of the great Maya race which followed the Itzas in the possession of the land and were in turn driven

ut by the two succeeding waves of racial immigra-
tion that preceded the coming of the Aztecs to
Mexico. There are to-day six distinct tribal divi-
sons among the Indians in Chiapas; the majority
of two of the largest tribes do not speak Spanish.
One of the tribes, the Lacandones, live according to
their primitive customs, use bows and arrows for
weapons, and have never recognized the authority
of the Mexican Government.

The work in Chiapas is unique, in the second
place, because it is not the work of any foreign missionary or movement which is directly subsidized by
foreign funds, but it is largely the work of the
people themselves. Rev. Newell J. Elliott, of
our Mission, has general supervision over the
state; he has planned the development of the field
and has worked out the guiding principles for the
growth of the Church, but his home is in Orizaba,
three and one half days distant by rail, and, with
his responsibilities in that section of Mexico, he
has obviously not been able to keep in close personal
contact with the congregations in Chiapas. The
local leader there is Rev. José Coffin, the son of
a Scotch father and a Mexican mother, a man of
striking and pleasing personality, who combines
the creative fire of the Latin with the stanch persist-
ence of the Scotch. The method is direct personal
work among and by the people themselves. At
first, persons are sent to explore a certain district;
then colporteurs with Bibles begin their work; then
teachers of catechism are sent. (Here we perceive
the Scotch influence at work.) The district which

has been known thus far as a field of missionary
action is now called a "mission," and the work i
carried on by native missionaries who hold meeting
in friendly homes until the time comes for the es
tablishment of a church group and the designatior
of a room or building as chapel. These new be
lievers must pass through a six months' period of
probation, and when this period of probation is
over, those who have conformed their lives to
Christ's teaching are received as full members of
the Church, and the congregation is considered as
a unit in the larger community of the Church as
a whole in Chiapas. In this way, in five years,
seventy-two church groups, large and small, have
been formed, including four large church centers,
twenty-three "chapels," twenty-four "missions,"
and twelve "missionary fields of action," with a
total communicant membership of 817 and with
more than 2,000 candidates waiting for admission.
In 1921, 400 children were baptized and 200 persons
were admitted to full membership. With the exception of Mr. Coffin, two thirds of whose salary
is paid by the Mission, all of the leaders in the
church are voluntary workers. There is no current subsidy from the Mission, aside from a small
sum for the travel expenses of Mr. Coffin, nor has
the mission thus far invested any money for
property.

On Saturday, November 18, at an afternoon session of the conference attended by representatives
of the Church from all sections of Chiapas, we
heard the direct reports of the work in the various

ortions of the state. Fifteen men from as many districts made reports; all of them had come at their own expense or through the gifts of their local groups. One of them had traveled eight days over the mountains to be present. The spirit of these men was most impressive as they gave their witness to the work of Christ in their communities and in their own lives. They continually laid stress upon the part each individual could play in bringing others to Christ. Some of the incidents which were related revealed true heroism; there is space to repeat only a single instance:

A year and a half ago, a Church member named Alvino Lopez, who lived near Tapachula, was threatened with death if he should continue to hold to the Protestant faith. One night he was shot and killed from ambush as he opened the door of his home. A memorial service was held there by the little congregation of twenty people. Afterwards they gathered at the Tapachula chapel on horse-back, and took a solemn oath with uplifted hands to be true to the Protestant faith, to preach the gospel, and, in memory of their fallen comrade, to win others to Christ. They had kept this pledge, and in the eighteen intervening months, in the face of persecution and threat of death, had brought 132 individuals into the Church. Such a spirit is invincible and during our days in Tapachula we saw abundant evidence of its many triumphs.

The work in Chiapas is exceptional, in the third place, because there a practical plan is being put into effect to develop Christian communities which

through ownership and cultivation of the land shal
become independent and self-supporting. W
visited one of these agricultural colonies, calle
Eisleben in memory of Martin Luther, which
numbering sixty-two families, had purchased on
thousand acres of land and was going forward suc
cessfully in this practical experiment. There
fiesta was held on November 17, the day after ou
arrival, when we saw some of the products of thi
community. A pavilion had been built, with up
rights of natural saplings and roofed with coco
nut-palm leaves. The platforms and the support
of the roof were festooned in a most wonderfu
fashion with the fruits of the region. Coconuts
pineapples, papayas, cacao pods, corn, oranges
bananas, and sugar cane dangled before us and
above us as we addressed the people. We noted
eighteen different varieties of fruit and vegetables
one of them, a huge cluster of coconuts, had an inscription which was typical of the spirit of the day
and of the practical and independent aims of the
agricultural center and of the Church:

" Within five years I will produce fuel, fiber,
soap, oil for food and lighting, and lubricant for
airplanes. Without exhausting the soil as do my
friends the corn and banana, I shall be giving fruit
to the Presbyterians at their second centennial in
2072 A.D." (Referring to the founding of the
Presbyterian Church in 1872.)

Finally we felt the work of the church in Chiapas was unique because of the exceptional warmth
and glow of its spirit of Christian fellowship and

devotion. That spirit was in evidence throughout every hour of the three days' conference: it showed in the welcome that was given us when we first arrived; it was apparent at the *fiesta* on the following day, in the services there, in the personal work carried on during all the functions of the day, in the rousing " *Vivas!* " given for the country and the Church, and in the chorus of voices uniting in " *Gloria y honor a Jesu-Cristo!* " It was present the next day in the conferences for the giving of reports and for meditation and prayer; it marked the public meetings Sunday morning, afternoon, and evening when we spoke of the " living water of Christ" that could bring new life to Mexico, to our Church, and to each one of us; and when we talked of missionary work in other parts of the world, in Siam, in the Philippines, and in China. It was audible when one of the members of the Church, out of deference to us, sang in English, " My country, 'tis of thee," and when with the national flag before us, we all sang, " *Mexico, mi Mexico.*" It was given clear expression in a statement read by Mr. Coffin at the final meeting on Sunday evening, in which he reviewed the work of the past and spoke of their hopes for the future; it was finally articulate in the farewell given to us when our train pulled out of Tapachula at five o'clock on Monday morning.

There are certain things which it is not wise or right for our Mission and Church to do for this work so well begun in Chiapas. Certainly nothing should be done which in any way will check or re-

tard the present tendencies toward self-propaga-
tion, self-government, and financial independence
Certain sections in the state, however, including
the non-Spanish speaking members of certain of
the Indian tribes, are not being reached. There is
a need for American missionaries who will set themselves to learn the Indian dialect and to carry the
gospel to them in their own language. Later, as
the church in Chiapas develops, there will be a need
of a training school for its younger leaders, and
American educators will be needed in this school
Funds will be required for the property for such a
school and certain limited investments could wisely
be made at once in order to help congregations in
the more important centers to purchase church
properties. Anyone who will invest life or money
here can be certain of a satisfying return.

Mr. Coffin closed his statement on Sunday night
with a verse from one of the hymns which we have
often sung together:

" Trabajad, trabajad, somos siervos de Dios;
Seguiremos la senda que el Maestro trazó;
Renovando las fuerzas con bienes que da,
El deber que nos toca, cumplido será! "

" To the work, to the work, we are servants of
        God,
    Let us follow the path that the Master has trod;
    With the balm of His counsel our strength to
        renew,
    Let us do with our might what our hands find
        to do."

Mr. Coffin gave a ringing emphasis to these closing words, and as we heard him speak, and as we thought of all that we had seen and heard of the work going forward under his brave and wise leadership, we resolved that anything which we as a Mission and as a Church could wisely do to support and sustain this work — anything that ought to be done — by the grace of God, would be done.

CHAPTER IX

A MEXICAN'S VIEW OF A PIONEER PROTES-TANT CHURCH IN SOUTHERN MEXICO

THE unique power and growth of the indigenous Church in Chiapas have been described in the preceding chapter. Reference was made to the striking address made by the leader in this movement, Rev. José Coffin, at the last session of the church *fiesta* in Tapachula. The Commission was so impressed by his words that they asked Mr. Coffin to write out what he had said. This he kindly consented to do and a translation of the address in part is here reproduced.

CHIAPAS AND OUR MISSIONARY WORK

The Presbyterian Church in Chiapas is a missionary movement and nothing else; but it is a movement whose reach it would still be premature to calculate.

I come before you to present some of the characteristics of this movement whose effect we know will reach across many generations, because we are living witnesses of one of those religious awakenings which the people themselves initiate and sustain until they accomplish the reforms and progress of their impelling motive.

Such progress has come through the method here employed. The method is none other than that of most patient personal work.

" One by one, little by little," is our slogan here, and in less than five years we have established seventy-two congregations where before there was not one.

How? Simply in this way: every new convert is made to feel that the chief aim of a member is to be a propagandist of the gospel and that in his period of probation, of at least six months, he ought to give testimony publicly in his conversations, establishing the family altar, making special visits to new persons and places, contributing his money to the work of the Church. There is hardly a member who has not brought several persons to the light before he himself has been baptized; in many cases the members have displayed heroic effort. The heroic congregations of San Cristobal, Las Casas, Chiapa del Corzo, and other congregations were established by candidates in their period of probation.

Our plan of evangelization of different points includes the following steps: First they are considered as " fields of missionary action " and are visited by persons who only explore the field, establishing the greatest possible number of points of contact; these are followed immediately by the catechism teachers and colporteurs, until public opinion has been formed, as one might say, in our favor; then we designate that field as a Mission, and it is attended to by native missionaries. These workers hold meetings from place to place in friendly homes, generally without any set form, continuing in this manner until these sympathizers believe that a formal meeting is opportune.

Immediately the pastor or an elder examines the new believers, who are thenceforth recognized officially and commence their six months of probation, unless the session should waive this or other detail of procedure.

This period of probation over, all those who have conformed their lives to the teachings of Jesus are received, and the rest are given one or two years of further probation in order to conform their lives. If, at the end of this time, they have not moralized their lives they are definitely rejected and the other sessions are notified so that they may not be deceived by false believers; the same is done in the case of anyone who is unworthy of Church fellowship.

When the new congregations are thus formed the Mission is raised to the standing of a chapel, a room for meeting is arranged for, a chaplain is named with his assistant, and a collector of funds who receives the offerings and renders an account to the treasurer of the session. Every chapel group may name the committees, commissions, and groups which it desires, but the officials as well as the members of these chapel groups have a vote simply as members of the church under the session whose rulings have the force of law in their jurisdiction. These lay preachers called native missionaries and chaplains, respectively, renew their appointment

ON THE WAY TO EL RANCHO DEL AGUILA

Left to right — D. H. Day, L. P. Van Slyke, A. W. Wolfe, J. B. Rodgers, W. R. Wheeler (*p. 20*).

every six months. These officials become the future sessions.

Our present organization consists of four sessions with twenty-three chapels, twenty-four Missions, and twelve missionary fields of action. The total number of communicants in full membership according to the latest statistics is 817. The amount collected for missions, benevolences, and construction forms a total of 2,141.80 pesos.

During the last synodical year we have performed eighty baptisms of children, received eighty-three adults, and performed seventy-six marriages.

But the beginning of Presbyterianism will go down in history as the real triumph of the agrarian ideal, which does not ruin the rich or give false hopes to the poor, because it is well within the law of respect for the rights of others. This is not opportunism or bad politics, but good sense; Chiapas will always be an agricultural state and the future of Presbyterianism is in the mountain and the valley. Ranch owners and laborers now as never before need, and are seeking far and wide, not so much people of initiative and ability as people of honesty, just the old honesty of Bible morals. In the face of this great need of the day only the austere Presbyterians have been able to make a reply in acts. This fact logically brought on the other necessity of establishing our brethren, so to speak, stimulating those who are not yet landowners to buy their own homes in the country or in the

towns, until if it is possible no family or individual
need depend on others for a livelihood. We, the
teachers of religion, do not have to give classes in
agricultural instruction in order to make sure that
the creed of the joyful Presbyterian peasant is expressed in three simple words — " Prayer, work,
and watchfulness."

The creed in practice glorifies God without ex-
ploiting either rich or poor, without cultivating
vice, laziness, or the crime which is so characteristic
of festival days.

One of the consequences of its adaptation to
circumstances has been the surprising facility in
finding volunteers for missionary work, men and
women of practical character, self-sacrificing to the
point of heroism and martyrdom, accustomed to
depend upon themselves and to direct others, strict
in discipline and orthodox in doctrine. So the wise
counsel of Rev. N. J. Elliott in 1919 that the
evangelization of Chiapas ought to be done princi-
pally by the Chiapanecos, stimulating them in spirit
and fact by frank coöperation, in the faith that they
understand their own people better than anyone
else; this prudent advice, I say, has been followed
to the letter.

As to our agrarian policy, I will simply say that
it realizes the dreams of one of our martyrs, the
humble Alvino Lopez, who in view of the suffering of the peasant families who had been driven by
the war to vagrancy, misery, prostitution, and sickness, initiated on his land an agricultural colony,
a few days before the hand of an assassin took him

rom us. But the idea has triumphed, for we have
'ourteen agrarian colonies, some of which are made
ıp of day laborers, others of renters, and others of
:mall property owners. Last year to celebrate the
'ourth centenary of the reform proclaimed by
Martin Luther, we established the colony of Eisle-
)en in which there are 130 hectares of good farming
.and, near the Pan-American Railroad's branch
ine to Suchiate, eighteen kilometers from Tapa-
:hula. The Company has sold us land at the rate of
.wo meters square for one centavo in the urban part
ınd six meters square for one centavo in the farm-
ng land. Although we are not so optimistic as one
)f our geologist friends who assures us that Eisleben lies over petroleum deposits, we are sufficiently
Presbyterian not to forget that Eisleben is a magnificent missionary point in a vast region on this
frontier.

Among the valuable testimonies which prove the
success of our particular system of colonization established in 1920 in Soconusco, I will cite the words
of the Secretary of Agriculture in an official report
rendered August 16, 1921, to the general office of
the Department in this zone:

" I note yours of the seventh instant to which I
add the documents relative to the colonization which
Señor José Coffin is carrying out in the state of
Chiapas. I have sent these documents to the Department of Colonization for the purpose of having
them duly studied and the points of benefit noted.
Thanking you, etc."

The General Agent referred to in this personal

letter dated November 8, 1921, honored me with
the following words:

" I was able to see the Subsecretary of Agriculture for the purpose of seeing what had come of
the plan of the Secretary for promulgating a
colonization law. I was informed they were about
to send a law of colonization to the Chamber of
Deputies in which it is planned to adopt your system for the agrarian colonies which have been
formed under the protection of the educational and
religious work of your Mission. (Signed by Civil
Engineer M. Castellanos Ruiz.) "

I must say here that we have not for a moment
solicited help from the government, much less have
we mixed in politics or party issues, but we have,
according to law, respectfully submitted reports
and data with all promptness and clearness.

Also we have not neglected the instruction of
children. Opportunely and according to necessity,
we have opened up rural schools and Bible schools
in connection with them. It is the duty of the
teachers in the day schools to help with the religious instruction of the children on Sunday. In
order technically to organize the educational work
on our field we have named a Presbyterian Committee of Education, which will unify all the elements of the four sessions in this important department of our work. I should say in passing that we
found all our systematic religious teaching on the
Shorter Catechism.

Now that I am speaking of our different departments, I must refer to one that is of capital im-

portance for us, and which corresponds to medical missions. We should not be real Presbyterians if we did not remember that since the time of Dr. Prevost, blessed among the blessed of God, and up to the time of Mr. Elliott and Señor Mirabal, our Church has represented the true beneficence of national medical evangelization. Here we have always included the medical outfit with the Bible. Without pretending to act as doctors, we have offered our humble help as nurses under the orders of regular physicians and at times the doctors have helped us generously. Perhaps you could understand later why at the present time the preachers accept the burden of the medical kit, but those who accompany us through the desert places where there are wild beasts, reptiles, and threatening microbes, or through populated districts where the people follow us with sticks and stones and knives and pistols, those who know that in Chiapas a small percentage of the population live in towns of importance and have access to medical help, will understand this. And the great majority who live in the country have only the quack doctors and the Indian medicine men (witches) who practice the superstitions of a thousand years ago. Because of all this we are calling aloud for medical missionaries to fight not only against sickness but also against its age-long ally, neglect! Yes, neglect, to which must be charged skin leprosy, among other great evils! We plead to God, to the Church, to your sympathy, brethren, to send us missionary doctors to teach hygiene, to give true medical instruction to thousands of your neighbors who were born and will die in this beautiful region where the two Americas meet, and where the eternal lullaby of two oceans is heard.

Gentlemen, although in the matter of ritual everyone has his own choice, we are, here in this farthest corner of our fatherland, celebrating the Jubilee of our Church; and this modest celebration has become an event because of the presence of these most worthy delegates whom our mother Church has lovingly sent from far-off lands. With the same pleasure with which we welcome them we give you another salutation. We ask of you to be the bearers of our fraternal regards to your noble Mission Board which represents the missionary power of our great Presbyterian family in the whole earth. Say to our great fraternity that under its offices we have raised up a people which will carry forward the blue standard of Scotch Presbyterianism, Catechism and all, in spite of the attacks of all the allies of Rome.

Brothers and Coworkers: To the memory of Procopio C. Diaz, who in 1885 began the literary propaganda in Tabasco and corresponded with friends in Pichucalco; to the memory of the colporteurs, who, like the humble Manuel M. Fernandez, did all they could; to the memory of him who thirty years ago had the great missionary vision of remote Chiapas, the renowned Dr. Arcadio Morales, whose last thoughts were for this field; to the memory of the Mexican Synod under whose auspices twenty years ago Mr. McDonald and wife, of

Livingstonian spirit, and Señor Rodríguez, of
Tuxtla Gutiérrez, came to preach the gospel here;
in honor of the veterans who are gone and those
who still live, as a testimony of our supreme faith
in the Church triumphant of the future, we have
made ours the words of the hymn:

" To the work! to the work! we are servants of
        God,
    Let us follow the path that the Master has trod;
    With the balm of His counsel our strength to
        renew,
    Let us do with our might what our hands find
        to do."

CHAPTER X

ACHIEVEMENT AND OPPORTUNITY IN JALAPA

Mexico City,
November 25, 1922

THE range of mountains which bounds the central plateau of Mexico on the east is pierced by two passes, through which it is possible to reach the lowlands bordering the Mexican Gulf. The city of Orizaba, which we visited on November 10 and 11, is situated on the railroad built through one of these passes; the city of Jalapa is located on the line which traverses the second valley. There we arrived the evening of the twenty-third and spent the following day visiting the city and our work before going on to Mexico City that night.

Jalapa is the capital of the state of Vera Cruz, a city of about 25,000 people, built on a mountain slope, with steep, narrow, winding streets paved with cobblestones that remind one of the streets of Clovelly, in Devonshire. But the city is typically Spanish, and there are some imposing governmental buildings that give it character and distinction. Every street is bounded by an unbroken line of stone and brick houses that stretch out like interminable prison walls. The illusion of enforced confinement is heightened by the barred windows which are so often present in the houses of Mexico.

The windows are long and cut low, so that an un-
obstructed view is given of the people within. The
women and girls who peer through these bars seem
like prisoners, and prisoners in one sense they have
been indeed, for they have been bound by fetters
of economic and ecclesiastical forging, from which
they are only now breaking free.

Jalapa is situated on the *Camino Real*, which was
the main thoroughfare of the Spanish conquerors
between Mexico City and Vera Cruz. Tradition
says that before the coming of the Spaniards, re-
lays of swift Indian runners passed over this trail,
carrying fish fresh from the bay at Vera Cruz to
the table of Montezuma. Jalapa, Orizaba, and
Vera Cruz make up the three centers of the Vera
Cruz Station of our Mission, and over this same
Camino Real messengers are passing to-day who
own allegiance to a King with a far wider realm
than that of which a Montezuma or a sixteenth
century Spanish sovereign would have dared to
dream.

Rev. and Mrs. H. A. Phillips are stationed in
Jalapa, with the responsibility of the oversight of
the work in the capital and also in the many neighboring towns and villages that look to this city as
their metropolitan center. We stayed at their
house overnight and with them inspected the new
church building which had been erected under Mr.
Phillips' supervision. An earthquake in 1920 had
destroyed the previous church building and certain
adjoining property. Funds were provided for the
erection of a new church, and the present struc-

ture, which has been built of reënforced concrete
is one of the two or three really attractive Presby
terian church buildings which we have seen in Mex
ico. We had a service in that church in the eve
ning, the pastor, Señor Vazquez, a full-blooded
descendant of the original Mexitl or Aztec Indians
presiding. The church needs an additional $1,00
to complete its building and there is need for th
securing of property for a school and residence
An adjoining lot next to the church might b
bought for this purpose if funds were available
There is need also of additional recruits to reën
force our single missionary family there.

In the afternoon we visited the chapel of th
Virgin de la Piedad out on the border of the city
In this chapel there is a picture believed to hav
healing power. It has been in the possession o
a certain Mexican family for two generations, and
the chapel in which it is contained has become th
Mecca for many sick and infirm. The walls o
the chapel were covered with pictures and inscrip
tions by those who had declared themselves to b
miraculously healed after they besought the hel
of the Virgin. In front of her picture was a motle
assortment of glass vases, candlesticks, and bowls
which presented the appearance of a secondhan
junk shop. Indians doffed their sombreros, a
they entered, to kneel on the pavement before th
picture and before this motley assortment of glass
ware, mothers brought their sick children, and
prayed for their recovery. The owner of the pic
ture, a frowsy, unkempt individual, stood an

watched these supplicants as they came and went, leaving some financial payment for the service they so confidently expected to receive.

We were reminded of similar scenes enacted before the picture of the " Black Christ," in a cathedral in Puebla. The picture had been festooned with white ribbons, placed there by those who, like these people of Jalapa, had come seeking the healing mercies which they thought could thus be gained. As we watched and thought of these things, we felt anew the pathos of such blind and ignorant devotion and the unescapable obligation which is placed upon those who know the Christian gospel in its purity and power to share the light and joy of that gospel with these people groping in the dark. The verses of Sidney Lanier which speak of the grace and beauty of the " Crystal Christ " took on a new meaning, and the words of that Christ rang in our ears with a new significance: " God is a Spirit: and they that worship Him must worship in spirit and truth."

CHAPTER XI

MEXICO CITY AND THE VALLEY OF MEXIC

En Route to YUCATAN,
December 8, 1922

"THE history of ancient Mexico is substantiall that of the Valley of Mexico, that beautift spot where once beat the heart of the great Azte Empire." So wrote Prescott in his unique histor of the conquest of Mexico; with almost equal trut it might be stated that the history of modern Mex ico and of the work of our Protestant Church, an especially of the Presbyterian branch of tha Church, is epitomized in the developments in tha same valley. In this letter I will try to give yo some of our general impressions of the city an valley, and of our work there, as these impression came to us during our stay from October 27 t November 1, and from November 25 to Decembe 8, in this interesting and historical center.

The Valley of Mexico is a vast basin, about fift miles long by forty miles broad, with an elevatio of 7,500 to 8,000 feet above sea level. The valle is thought to be the one-time floor of an extinc volcano whose walls were the surrounding moun tains. Within this valley there were once five grea lakes, mountain-locked, and formerly dotted by th " Floating Gardens " of the Aztecs. These lake have dwindled in size so that Lake Texcoco, nea

Mexico City, alone remains of appreciable extent. The valley is drained by a canal and a tunnel cut through the mountain range, a work that was attempted by the early Aztecs, but not completed until the régime of Porfirio Diaz.

The valley is completely surrounded by mountain ramparts, with Popocatepetl and Iztaccihuatl standing, sentinel-like, in the southeast distance. When we viewed this scene, it was easy to understand why the migrating peoples who had swept down in successive waves from the north had decided to go no farther, but had chosen to settle here and build their cities and homes in this watered and protected valley.

Three of these migratory invasions are of special interest: that of the Toltecs, of the Aztecs, and that of the Spanish conquerors.

The Toltecs came to the Mexican valley probably as early as the seventh century of our era. They built their capital city of Tula, some fifty miles north of Mexico City, and other cities nearer the present capital. The ruins of certain of these cities are of special archæological and religious interest to-day. On December 2, we visited one of them, San Juan Teotihuacan, " The City of the Gods," about thirty miles from Mexico City. Two great pyramids, the Pyramid of the Sun and the Pyramid of the Moon, the former equaling in extent the largest of the pyramids in Egypt, are here. Near by are the ruins of the stone houses of an ancient city; beneath its very foundation, recent excavations have revealed other houses which belong to an epoch even more ancient. In similar fashion, two temples have been discovered, one superimposed upon another, the sculptured gargoyles and decorations indicating two distinct eras of civilization and art. But most impressive of all is the great many-staired altar that stands within a vast rectangular enclosure, which in turn is flanked on three sides by twelve lesser altars, four on each side of the enclosure, with the double temple at the farther end. There is a symmetry and a precision about the whole plan that is most impressive, which recalls the beauty and inspired simplicity of Hellenic art; there is also something of the spirit there that surrounds the Temple and Altar of Heaven in Peking. No one can stand on this ancient altar in San Juan Teotihuacan, " The City of the Gods," under the beautiful Mexican sky, and not feel that here, just as in Athens, were a people who were seeking after " God, if haply they might feel after Him and find Him."

The record of the Aztecs is written indelibly on Mexico. The very name of the country comes from their patron war god, Mexitl. The seal of the nation reproduces the eagle and the snake which were the prophetic symbols of the appointed place for the building of the Aztec capital. Guided by this sign, they stopped on their southward journey, and on the margin of Lake Texcoco laid the foundations for their chief city, Tenochtitlan. This was in 1325, and for nearly two centuries their empire dominated the continent. There they built their temple to the war god, Huitzilopochtli, and, in

THE MEXICANS GREET THE AMERICAN MISSIONARY IN THE MOUNTAINS OF OAXACA (*p. 20*).

1486, dedicated it with the sacrifice of 20,000 human victims. In the National Museum is the wonderful Calendar Stone of this people, a mammoth circular block of basaltic porphyry, twelve feet in diameter and weighing twenty-four tons, upon which are marked a sundial and the seasons and months and days of the Aztec calendar, significant proof of their high level of culture and civilization. There, too, is the image of Huitzilopochtli, which at one time stood upon the top of Teocalli, and was ignominiously tumbled down therefrom by the disrespectful soldiers of Cortes. In a suburban town where stood another temple of Huitzilopochtli, which gave its name to the village, is now located a fine country club and golf links, the Aztec name of the district being transformed to the more peaceful and pronounceable Spanish version of Churubusco. In the museum, sculptured figures and faces of Toltecs and Aztecs and their forerunners bear striking resemblances to similar relics in Egypt, China, and Japan, and seem to bear out the theory that the original racial stream of Mexico came both from North America and from Eastern Asia. Mexico was a portion of the so-called New World, but it was old long before the coming of the Europeans to its shores. The familiar lines concerning its ancient glories are indeed true:

" World wrongly called the new! this claim was old
    When first the Spaniards came, in search of gold.
    Age after age its shadowy wings had spread,
    And man was born and gathered to the dead;

Cities arose, ruled, dwindled to decay,
Empires were formed, then darkly swept away;
Race followed race, like cloud-shades o'er the
    field,
The stranger still to strangers doomed to yield.
The last grand line that swayed these hills and
    waves,
Like Israel, wandered long 'mid wilds and caves,
Then settling in their Canaan, cities reared,
Fair Science wooed, a milder God revered,
Till to invading Europe bowed their pride,
And pomp, art, power, with Montezuma died."

In 1519, Hernando Cortes landed at Vera Cruz, and after two years of bloody warfare, Tenochtitlan surrendered to the Spaniard. For three centuries, the Spanish flag floated over Mexico. With the soldiers came the priests of the Roman Catholic Church. One of the first acts of Bishop Señor Zumarraga was the collection of the manuscripts and paintings deposited in the Texcoco library and their public destruction, thus attempting to do away with the writings of false religion, but, incidentally, accomplishing the destruction of records of incalculable value to science and history.

In 1531, ten years after the surrender of the Aztec sovereign, according to the popular tradition, appeared the vision and picture of the Virgin of Guadalupe. An Indian of the poorer class was passing the rocky hill of Tepeyac, near Mexico City, when the Virgin Mary appeared to him and told him of her desire to have a church built in that place, and that this desire should be communicated to the bishop. Señor Zumarraga and the other church leaders proved skeptical, and after two further visions, on her third appearance, on December 12, as a proof of her reality, the Virgin caused a garden of beautiful roses to appear on the crest of the rocky hill of Tepeyac. At her command, the Indian gathered the flowers in his mantle, or *tilma,* to take to the bishop, and when the mantle was unrolled, upon it they saw painted a picture of the Virgin. This picture on the sacred *tilma* is said to be in existence to-day and is exhibited in the cathedral of Guadalupe which has been built at the base of the hill of Tepeyac. The Indians have identified the Virgin of Guadalupe with their own Tonantzin, goddess of earth and corn and their special protectress, and throughout Mexico and especially among the Indian population, the Virgin is regarded as the divine patroness of the nation. Miguel Hidalgo carried her banner when he proclaimed the independence of Mexico on the night of September 5, 1810; through such association, her influence is both religious and nationalistic. The cathedral and town of Guadalupe are the Mecca of the Roman Catholic Indians, and on December 12, the anniversary of the appearance of the picture of the Virgin, tremendous crowds visit the shrine.

We went to Guadalupe on December 3, and as soon as we entered the village, we felt the air of emotional fervor and excitement. The cathedral was jammed with Indians, the men in blankets and sombreros, and the women with shawls and staring, round-eyed babies, each of the men and women kneeling with a tall lighted candle in their hands. The interior of the cathedral was dark, and the flickering flame of the candles cast an eerie light over the dusky faces and huddled bodies of the Indians. Before them was the high altar, built of marble and bronze, with the sacred *tilma* and painting of the Virgin enclosed in a gold frame. Below the picture was the gigantic kneeling figure of a priest, cut in marble, whose silent, gray form added a grotesque and sepulchral touch to the scene. Above, through two windows near the roof, came two shafts of clear, warm sunlight that streamed through the murky semidarkness below, bringing a message of light and peace from the fair heavens above. So, I have seen the sunlight pierce the gloom of a Buddhist temple in the Far East, adding a new and strange luster to the image of the " Light of Asia "; and thus I have seen the torches borne by Confucianist devotees at the spring festivals in China fade out in the clear morning light of a new day's dawn.

After viewing the ceremony in the cathedral, we visited the chapel on the hill where the roses are said to have bloomed. Then we descended to the chapel of the well, at the foot of the hill. In the floor of one of the rooms of this chapel is a well of water which is regarded by the Indians as possessing healing and medicinal properties. The spring of water is said to have gushed forth at the appearance of the Virgin and we found the room

crowded with Indians seeking to dip up water
from the well which they might carry with them.
As we watched, we heard the strains of music in
the adjoining auditorium of the chapel. There, we
saw a dozen Indians, men and women, with elab-
orate feather headdresses, engaged in a rhythmical
dance to the strange music of banjo-like instruments played by two of the Indians as they danced.
Three of the men held up banners on which were
pictures of the Virgin of Guadalupe, topped with
crosses. Thus the old Indian impulses to worship
by dance and music had been incorporated, or at
least tacitly approved, as a part of the ritual of the
local Roman Catholic Church, just as Buddhism
admits into its pantheon all gods and rites that have
a vitality of their own.

In this valley, with its Toltec, Aztec, and Spanish background, and on the very site of the ancient
city of Tenochtitlan, the modern City of Mexico
stands to-day. The Spanish rulers have been gone
for nearly a century; during the past hundred
years, many new forces have been at work. Most
visible are the signs of French and American influence. The architecture of palace and church and
residence is still predominantly Spanish, but many
of the beauties of parks and avenues in origin are
French. Maximilian laid out the magnificent
street, Paseo de la Reforma, with its circles
(*glorietas*), and its statues and its winding course
through the beautiful Chapultepec forest, with its
lakes and inlets and inviting paths under its great
cypresses. Here is a second Bois de Boulogne,

and above the wood, on a bold cliff, like that of Stirling Castle, stands the castle of Chapultepec, the former residence of the French emperor and more recently of the Mexican presidents. Almost within the shadows of this castle and along a prolongation of the Paseo de la Reforma, enterprising Americans have marked out modern city blocks, and are beginning the construction of residences and bungalows of approved California pattern. Trolley cars of American make and speed carry one out to the beautiful suburban villages of the district. In the city itself, there are said to be 40,000 automobiles. Fords and Packards vie with one another in these crowded streets. The population of the city is estimated to be more than half a million with nearly three quarters of a million within the Federal District. After traveling through the country regions, where the standards of living seem so low, one marvels at the evidence of apparent wealth and financial activity in this metropolis, where the commercial spirit of one of our twentieth century American cities seems to be at work in a European setting and an environment of long ago.

The focal point of the past history and present life of Mexico and of the capital, has been and is in the main plaza of the city, called La Plaza de la Constitucion or, more popularly, the Zocalo. On the site of the Teocalli, on the north side of the plaza, now stands the great Cathedral of Mexico, the corner stone of which was laid in 1573. On the east side of the plaza is the Senate. Above its

central doorway hangs the famous liberty bell first
rung by the patriot Hidalgo in 1810 and rung
again each year on the anniversary of that September night. On the south side of the Zocalo
stands the Municipal Palace, occupying the site of
the former residence of the Aztec commanders.
In this square raged the final battles between the
Aztecs and the invading Spaniards. There, in
1822, Agustín de Iturbide was proclaimed Emperor of Mexico. The American flag floated above
the National Palace in 1847 and it was followed in
1863 by the Tricolor of France. Here, in 1867,
General Porfirio Diaz was first greeted as a national leader, and here, in 1911, his resignation,
demanded by Madero, was made public. The full
force of the *Decena Trágica* (tragic ten days), at
the time of the entrance of General Huerta into the
capital, culminating in the death of President Madero, was here felt. From this square, President
Carranza set out, in 1920, on the tragic journey
which was to end with his death. And here President Obregon was inaugurated and began his present term of office. And finally, in this place, we
were afforded a glimpse of the quick flaring action
of the Mexican populace, which has made possible
so many tragedies in the comparatively short
history of their existence as an independent nation.

When we met for the Mission conference, the
last week in November, in Mexico City, we found
that the city had been without water for nearly ten
days. The reason for the failure in the municipal
water supply was never clearly stated, but what-

ever its original cause, the resentment of the peopl
of the city grew more and more strong. On th
afternoon of Thanksgiving Day, November 30
a large crowd collected and marched throug!
the streets, protesting against the lack of water
The crowd entered the plaza and drew up befor
the municipal palace, about seven o'clock, just a
Dr. Rodgers and I arrived by street car from th
suburb of San Ángel. The crowd made a rush a
the palace where the municipal authorities wer
thought to be; the soldiers on guard opened fire
and the next moment we found ourselves in th
crowd of frightened people who were seeking cove
behind every possible object, including the stree
cars and statues in the plaza. As the firing continued, we worked our way across the plaza and so
into a side street. The crowd returned to the attack later in the evening; eleven of them wer
killed and sixty wounded in the fighting, and th
palace was set on fire in the *mêlée*. That night we
heard groups of men going through the streets
crying, " *Agua! Agua!* " (water! water!) but there
was no fighting outside the Zocalo. Such an incident was exceptional, however, and from our observation of conditions in Mexico as a whole, we
believe life there to be as safe, at least, as in New
York City.

In this pulsating and historic city and valley, the
work of our Church was begun fifty years ago.
We were impressed at once by the strategic position of our largest congregation, called *El Divino
Salvador*. During all this period, until the day of

is death this past year, Señor Arcadio Morales was pastor, and in that time built up the church and won a place of leadership and influence throughout the whole country. The church of San Pedro and San Pablo is also situated in Mexico City and the A. R. Wolfe Memorial Church is located in the suburban district of Tacubaya. At Coyoacán, a suburban town about five miles from the center of the city, is our preparatory school for boys, the only Protestant school for boys in the whole city and Federal District. Coyoacán is older, historically, than Mexico City; there Cortes had his first headquarters. The house in which he lived four hundred years ago, is still standing there to-day. Mr. and Mrs. R. A. Brown, and Rev. and Mrs. Bancroft Reifsnyder live in Coyoacán, and Mr. Brown as director and member of the faculty and Mr. Reifsnyder as supervisor of evangelistic work are carrying a large load of responsibility and service. The Southern Presbyterians are united with us in the school, Mr. R. C. Morrow being a member of the faculty from their constituency. There are over 100 boys enrolled, seventy-three of them being boarders. Señor E. Z. Perez is the pastor of the Coyoacán Church, which meets in the beautiful McMurtrie Memorial Chapel on the school campus, where the congregation of Coyoacán and San Ángel students is most inspiring.

At San Ángel, a beautiful suburb about a mile from Coyoacán, is the Girls' Primary and Normal School. It was a joy to see the beautiful old trees and ample grounds surrounding our school there.

Miss Lucile L. Sage and Miss Florence M. Beatty are our representatives on the faculty, with Miss Alice McClelland from the Southern Presbyterian Mission. Miss Ivy V. Yeaworth, a newly appointed member of the Mission, is doing part-time work there during her period of language study. Nearly one hundred girls are there, most of them being boarders. In January, Miss Mary F. Turner will come from Vera Cruz to be the *Directora* of San Ángel. The death in 1922 of Miss Jennie Wheeler, who, for so many years, first at Saltillo and then at San Ángel, had served the girl students of our Church, and who had won a unique place in their hearts, was a blow to all who knew and loved her; but the work of the school is going forward in her spirit of courage and devotion.

In the city is the Union Theological Seminary, in which our Church is coöperating, with Dr. William Wallace, Chairman of the Executive Committee of the Mission, as our representative on the faculty. In the city, also, is the playground and social center, called *El Faro,* under the direction of Rev. Charles Petran, who is also the treasurer of the Mission. It was at Mr. Petran's suggestion that the American residents in Mexico City decided to contribute a community playground to the city and nation as their gift at the celebration of the centennial of Mexican independence, and this playground is a living symbol of the American spirit of altruism expressed in practical service to the children of the community. The Mission is also coöperating in a union press and bookstore and in the publication of a union weekly paper in which eight denominations are united, so that it represents the Protestant cause as a whole in Mexico.

There is no question of the strategic importance of the work of our Church in the city and Federal District, and of the notable and abiding service which has been rendered; there is also no question but that the Church and Mission need reënforcements and additional equipment, if the opportunities for the fullest and widest service are not to be lost. Eight missionaries are trying to do justice to the work of a girls' primary and normal school, of a boys' preparatory school, of a theological seminary, of a press and periodical, of a social center, and of direct evangelism in the capital and metropolitan district with a population of three quarters of a million. The standards of school, press, and Church cannot be maintained at the right level of efficiency, and the many individuals needing personal help and guidance cannot be served by such a limited force. Surely the challenge and opportunity of service in this historic and picturesque valley where once beat the heart of the Aztec empire and where beats no less the heart of Mexico to-day, will be heard and answered by the young men and women of our Church in America.

The need for new life comes first; but there is also a need that cannot be ignored for additional property and equipment, if this life is to be invested in the most serviceable way. The church building of *El Divino Salvador* is well located, but there

are no rooms in this former convent hall for socia
activities and classes for the young people of the
church. The Mexican Presbyterian Church i
planning to build in 1926 a cathedral church in the
city which will be worthy of the Presbyterian cause
in Mexico, and the Church in the United State,
should have a share in this building. The schoo
at Coyoacán, the only Protestant school for boy
in the city and Federal District, has only a chape
and a recitation hall and one faculty residence a
permanent property; parents of prospective stu
dents, after viewing the present temporary dormi
tories, one of the halls being built of adobe and al
of them being most inadequate, have sent thei
boys elsewhere. New dormitories for the student
and residences for the faculty members are needed
at once. At the San Ángel school there is no as
sembly hall for chapel exercises and for the gath
erings of the students and of visitors; at the com
mencement exercises, held one December evening
the graduating class and the audience were forced
to sit in a cold, unprotected corridor of the court
yard, a circumstance which robbed the evening
of much of its value and impressiveness. I wisl
that some of the people in the United States who
are interested in the education and service of young
people could have watched those girls, in thei
white graduating dresses, trying to ignore the
cold and dampness and to carry off the occasion
in the appropriate commencement manner. By
their support of the Christian education of the
youth of Mexico, Americans can truly reveal the

pirit of neighborliness and of inspired and inspiring helpfulness to a near-by nation that deeply
eeds such encouragement and help.

From November 26 to December 3, the Church
nd Mission, celebrated in Mexico City the Jubilee
f Presbyterian work in Mexico. The annual
Mission meeting was held from November 28 to
December 7, and representatives of the Mission
ere in attendance at the sessions of the Jubilee.
The meeting for prayer on the first day of the
Mission's annual conference was most impressive.
We had come from far-away points in the United
States and from isolated and lonely stations in
Mexico, and we were joined in fellowship with one
nd another and with Christ. He seemed very
ear to us that morning and all through the confer-
nce, and at the closing communion service. He
eemed to speak through those who spoke at the
Jubilee sessions of Mission and Church, as the
vents of the past fifty years were reviewed and the
oming half century was faced. In the final meet-
ng, Dr. Arellano, a veteran in the service of the
Church, led the memorial service for those who had
gone on into the larger service of the life beyond.
The church was decorated with roses and as he
named each of the men and women who had died,
he dropped a single flower at our feet. So they, be-
ng dead, yet spoke to all of us there assembled;
and I believe their voices will reach beyond the Rio
Grande to the hearts of those in our homeland
who possess the gifts of life and means to answer
their undying summons and appeal.

CHAPTER XII

YUCATAN AND THE PRECIOUS JEWELS
OF MÉRIDA

On steamer from PROGRESO,
December 19, 1922

ON December 8, the day after the close of th
Mission meeting, we left Mexico City to g
to Yucatan.

The Yucatan Peninsula forms the toe of th
Mexican boot which is pointed eastward toward
Cuba and the West Indies as if in the act of scat
tering these islands by a violent thrust over the
Caribbean Sea. The population of the states of
Yucatan and Campeche and of the territory of
Quintana Roo, which make up the peninsula, is
roughly half a million, with 400,000 in Yucatan
85,000 in Campeche, and 15,000 in the little known
and unsettled territory of Quintana Roo. The inhabitants of the peninsula are largely Maya Indians, descendants of the great race which first settled
there nearly 2,000 years ago. Ruins of their ancient
cities at Uxmal and Chichen-Itza are still visible
and in the words of their discoverer, J. L. Stephens.
who first made them known to the world in 1841:
" These remains are different from the works of
any other known people, there being nothing in
Europe like them. They are of a new order and

84

ALFONSO SOSA, A PROTESTANT EVANGELIST

MARTIN LOPEZ, THE COMPANION OF SOSA

PROTESTANT VICTIMS OF AN ATTACK BY A ROMAN CATHOLIC VILLAGE MOB (*Ch. IV*).

ntirely and absolutely anomalous." On his fourth
nd last voyage in 1502, Columbus picked up a
anoe off the Yucatan coast which was filled with
Yucatecos, and brought the first word of these
people to the rest of the world. It was not until
517, however, that Europeans landed on the Yuca-
an mainland; Fernández de Córdoba in that year
explored the coast as far as Campeche. Yucatan
was thus the first portion of the Mexican continent
to be made known to Europeans. To-day, its
people are among the most progressive of any of the
Mexican inhabitants. The chief industry is the
growth of henequen, or sisal, which, in its finished
product, makes up into a rough twine much in
demand in certain sections of the United States.
Ninety-eight per cent of the income of the state of
Yucatan is derived from the sale of this product.

The peninsula has no connection by railroad with
the Mexican mainland and is reached by boats sailing from the port of Vera Cruz to the port of Progreso. We embarked on December 9, our boat
making the trip in thirty-six hours. These ships
of the Ward Line sail originally from New York
and make successive stops at Havana, Progreso,
Vera Cruz, and Tampico.

The first glimpse of the Yucatan coast resembles
that of China at the mouth of the Yangtse as it appears to the traveler approaching from the sea.
The land is flat and level and our experiences in
the transportation by tender made me think of similar trips from Woosung to Shanghai. Mérida, the
capital and chief city of Yucatan, is fifty minutes

by rail from Progreso. As we traveled over the Yucatan plain, we felt a curious lightness and expansion of spirit, that apparently came from the fact that for the first time in two months we were in a locality that was not surrounded and hemmed in by mountain walls. The first impression of Mérida City was most pleasing. Its streets are wide and clean and well-paved; the houses are well-built and give evidence of the prosperity of their owners; there are no factories to darken their white walls, and the total impression is that of the legendary "Spotless Town," whose virtues are extolled in certain sections of the United States.

Our Mission has representatives stationed at the city of Campeche, the capital of the state of the same name, five hours by rail from Mérida, and in Mérida itself. Campeche is a city of 20,000 people built on the shores of the Yucatan Gulf. It was a well-known objective of the pirates and buccaneers of the Spanish Main and portions of the stone wall which was built as a defense around the city are still visible. Rev. and Mrs. L. C. Schaumburg and Miss Etta McClung are stationed in this city and have the responsibility for the supervision of the work in outlying districts and in other centers of the state. The work is still in its pioneer stages; our missionaries live in rented quarters; the little congregation meets in a rented house; and there is no permanent property for church or for school. Already, however, our missionaries and Church members are making friendly contacts with the people of the town and Mr. Schaumburg was

greeted with unmistakable cordiality wherever he
went.

In the state of Yucatan, there are four main
centers of work: Mérida, Progreso, Muna, and
Ticul. We visited all but Muna and took part in
the services in these various churches, carrying a
message of greeting from their Mexican brethren
to the north and from our own Church in the
United States.

In the city of Mérida, our work is going forward
in a well-balanced way, in church and social service
and school. Rev. and Mrs. J. T. Molloy have the
special responsibility of the social work there; Miss
Eunice Blackburn and Miss Elfreda McLennan
are the American teachers in the Turner-Hodge
School for Girls, Miss Blackburn carrying the responsibility of the directorship. Señor Blanco is
pastor of the local church, which has a membership
of 230 and which, under his leadership, is doing fine
service. Bible and reading rooms, under the supervision of the Molloys, are helping to reach certain
classes of people who would not otherwise be
served. The school we found most inspiring. The
faculty and students are housed in what was formerly the residence of a wealthy hacienda owner,
who had built a mammoth house, of seventeen
great rooms, with twenty-foot ceilings, ranged
about a beautiful *patio* in the center. There are
125 students there, two thirds of them being girls,
and we shall never forget the picture which they
presented in the Spanish setting of this ample
mansion. The Spanish names of some of these

children are most attractive: Angelita, Gloria
Natalia, Margarita, Maria, and Mercedes were
there enrolled. The *patio* was full of roses and
these children seemed like living flowers as they
gathered in the sunlight of the courtyard. Some
of them had come from low and squalid surroundings; they seemed full of happiness and the light-
heartedness of well-protected freedom; as we
watched them, and thought of the environment to
which they would return after leaving the school
and of the terrible toll that Mexican women still
have to pay because of the present standards of society and its unchecked evils, we could not but wish
that by some miraculous process they might be
kept in such a state of blessed innocence and joy.
That consummation can be only when Christ's
spirit and principles are regnant throughout Mexico.

Our missionaries and Church leaders in Mérida,
with great courage and patience, are laying the
foundations for the coming Kingdom of God. But
they, too, need reënforcements in equipment and
personnel. The able pastor of the local church is
forced to live in quarters which have been a menace
to himself and his family. The church has sub-
scribed half of the cost of a new manse and our
Mission hopes to give an equivalent amount. In
time a new church building will be required, as the
present one in certain seasons is stifling. Property
should be secured for the Bible and reading rooms,
which are in rented quarters, and especially should
the opportunity be grasped of purchasing the prop-

erty in which the school is now housed, which is on
the market for $50,000, half of the cost of its build-
ings only twenty years ago. Two additional
teachers are needed at once, as the burden of work
in this large school is too great for two American
girls to carry alone. A woman who can do social service in the city is needed and the expanding
work of evangelism will soon require another ordained man to coöperate with Dr. Molloy.

The churches in Yucatan were the last which we
visited in Mexico. Since crossing the northern
border on October 20, we had visited fourteen
large cities and centers of work, from the boundary
of Texas on the north to the borders of Guatemala
on the south. In his interpretation of one of our
speeches at Mérida, Dr. Wallace spoke of the work
there as being the *brocha de oro* (" brooch of gold,"
a favorite Mexican expression of approbation), in
the long chain of Presbyterian churches which we
had visited. As we met in the church that morning,
we heard the little children singing in Spanish the
hymn " Precious Jewels." I remember listening
to that hymn as a small child, when I was being
sung to sleep. In my own home, with my own two
small boys, on the day that I left for Mexico, we
sang that same hymn. Mérida was truly the
brocha de oro of our work in Mexico, but the jewels
in that brooch were the children whom we had seen
in school and in church. As we sailed away from
Progreso, on December 18, and as we saw the Mexican shore fading on the horizon, the words of that
hymn echoed clearly in our ears:

" *Jesus de los cielos*
  Al mundo bajó,
  En busca de joyas
  Que amante compró.

Coro: " *Los niños salvados*
  Serán como el sol,
  Brillando en la gloria
  Del Rey Salvador."

" The Christ from the heavens
  To earth did come down
  In search of the jewels
  He bought for His crown.

Chorus: " The children, the saved ones,
  Shall shine as the sun,
  They'll dwell in His glory,
  By Christ they were won."

Of such is the Kingdom of heaven in Mexico,
and happy indeed, are all those who can have a
part in the bringing in of that Kingdom.

CHAPTER XIII

OUTLINE HISTORY OF THE MEXICO MISSION

THE work of the Presbyterian Church in Mexico was officially begun in Mexico City in 1872. Dr. Henry C. Thomson has written of his early experiences in Mexico as one of the Presbyterian pioneers:

" It was my fortune to have been a member of a party of missionaries that sailed from New York City on September 10, 1872, on a steamer bound for the Mexican shores. Upon reaching Vera Cruz, the party gathered together for an earnest hour of prayer and supplication, that our work in this new land to which we had come might carry with it the blessings of almighty God.

" Our experiences on reaching the City of Mexico were various, and I well remember how we listened to a sermon preached in Spanish by Brother Rodríguez without understanding any part of it as we knew so very little or nothing at all of the language. We found that the British Bible Society had a well-organized Bible House and were distributing the Bible and parts of it among the natives. Also the American Bible Society had its work actively carried out by placing large numbers of Bibles on each steamer bound for Mexico, with especial orders for them to be distributed to as many as would freely wish to take them."

Work had been begun informally in 1852, radiating from Brownsville, Texas, as a center, and from Matamoros, opposite Brownsville. This work was under the direction of Miss Melinda Rankin. In her book entitled *Twenty Years Among the Mexicans* Miss Rankin reproduces many an interesting scene in this initial Protestant service on behalf of the people of Mexico. Miss Rankin crossed the border for this work in 1865, antedating by five years the entrance of the first missionary organizations, the Baptist Home Missionary Society, followed in 1871 by the Friends, who sent a missionary to Tamaulipas. Miss Rankin's work in Mexico was eventually transferred to the Congregational Church. The description of her experience in securing the first funds for her school in Brownsville has a message and a meaning for modern missionaries who are trying also to initiate new work and to find financial support and their Board's approval of that work:

" Leaving New Orleans, I went to Louisville, Ky., and was kindly received. As the churches were engaged in making their annual contributions to other objects I received no present aid, but was promised that at some future time they would assist me in my enterprise. I then went on to Philadelphia, arriving March 4, 1853, at two o'clock in the morning. At nine o'clock of the same morning I was wending my way to the rooms of the Presbyterian Board of Education, with a letter of intro-

luction from Rev. Dr. Hill, of Louisville, to the
secretaries, Dr. Chester and Dr. Van Rensselaer.
With these reverend gentleman I had to pass another severe and trying ordeal. All the difficulties
of the enterprise were again brought forward, and
paraded with considerable embellishment. I met
them with arguments which I thought ought to
have weight, but they seemed to make little impression upon either of the gentlemen, particularly
upon Dr. Chester. He seemed determined that my
enterprise should prove a failure. After talking
some time, without making any apparent impression favorable to the cause, I arose and said:
' Gentlemen, I leave the responsibilities of the
proper education of the youth of that portion of
the country upon your hands. I have done what I
can, and henceforth my skirts are clear of the
criminal negligence of leaving the beloved youth
of the Rio Grande Valley to the baleful influence
of foreign popery.' Dr. Chester immediately arose
to his feet, and with much emphasis, said: ' I am
not going to take the Rio Grande upon my
shoulders, you are the one to bear that burden.
We have fully tested your proper understanding
of the difficult enterprise, and your ability in carrying it forward. We are now ready to inquire of
your wants.' I replied, ' I must have money.'
' How much,' said he, ' do you want of us? ' I
felt quite subdued and modestly replied, ' Two or
three hundred dollars.' He replied: ' You must
not leave Philadelphia with less than five hundred.
If the Board of Education does not see fit to give

you two hundred Dr. Van Rensselaer and I will pay it out of our own pockets, and the remaining three hundred I will put you in the way of obtaining from the Presbyterian churches of the city.' "

Soon after the war of 1846, Dr. J. M. Prevost, of an old Huguenot family in Philadelphia, who had served as a surgeon in the American Army in Mexico, settled in Zacatecas, then one of the chief mining centers in the central table-land of Mexico. While accumulating a fortune, he preached the gospel, and for over forty years was known as the " Protestant Bishop," the wise counselor of a succession of missionaries who manned this Station.

In 1873 work was formally opened up in Zacatecas; in 1878, in San Luis Potosí; and in 1884, in Saltillo. These formed the Northern Mexico Mission. Another Mission was opened up in the South, with Mexico City as its center, there being at that time no railways connecting the North and South. Rev. N. N. Hutchinson opened up work in Mexico City in 1873, and was succeeded by Dr. Milton Greene. Under these missionaries, Presbyterian congregations were established in the states of Yucatan, Tabasco, Vera Cruz, Michoacán, and Guerrero. In 1894, Chilpancingo and Zitácuaro were made Mission stations; in 1897, Jalapa; Yucatan in 1911; and Oaxaca in 1919. All this southern territory formed the Southern Mission, until the two Missions were united in 1894. In 1907, the work in Aguascalientes, which had been carried on independently since 1897 by the Mission of the Cumberland Presbyterians, through the union of this

Church with our own in the States, now came under our Board.

A girls' school had been established by Miss Jennie Wheeler in the city of Monterey in 1888. In 1890 this school was moved to Saltillo. In 1907, Miss Mary F. Turner organized a school in Aguascalientes under the Presbyterian Board, this school having originally been a part of the work of the Cumberland Board. In 1897 a boys' school was established in the Federal District, and later a girls' school, known as Posadas, which was afterward called San Ángel. A mission press had been organized, that printed a periodical called *El Faro* — and did other printing for the Mission and Church. Its work was under the direction of Rev. C. A. Petran.

In the Annual Report covering 1914, the Mission reported eight principal stations, seventy-seven outstations, with a total of nineteen missionaries and a native force of 111. The total number of communicants was put at 3961.

This was the situation when at the capture of Vera Cruz by the American forces on April 21, 1914, all American missionaries were ordered from the country. The enforced cessation of mission work gave an opportunity for the restudy and redistribution of the representatives and responsibilities of the various Mission Boards in that country. There had been much overlapping and duplication of effort, and the disturbed conditions gave an opportunity for wiser adjustments. A conference of missionaries and of representatives

of practically all the Boards involved, was held at
Cincinnati from June 30 to July 1, 1914, and an
agreement concerning the redistribution of territory was drawn up and was referred to the various
Missions and Boards concerned. For details
concerning the conference and its results, see
Chapter XIV.

The period of revolution, dating from Novem-
ber, 1910, was a stormy one for the people of
Mexico, including, of course, the members of our
Church. A brief outline of the events from the
fall of Diaz, in 1910, to the election of General
Obregon, in September, 1920, prepared by the
Pan-American Union, indicates the turbulence of
that time:

" 1. The fall of Diaz in 1910, which was due to
discontent engendered by the granting of excessive
privileges.

" 2. The Madero régime, 1911–1913, which failed
because of attempted compromise with conservatives and reactionaries.

" 3. The Huerta régime, February 19, 1913, to
July 15, 1914, which began with the murder of
Madero and Suarez, and became a military dic-
tatorship.

" a. United States occupation of Vera Cruz,
April, 1914, to November, 1914.

" b. Refusal of the United States to recognize a government which gained its power
through intrigue and assassination.

" c. United States advises its nationals to
withdraw from Mexico.

" d. President Wilson's policy of 'watchful waiting.'

" e. United States lends aid to the Constitutionalist revolution under Carranza.

" f. 'A B C powers' mediate, as a result of which Huerta is eliminated.

" 4. Carranza régime, July, 1915, to May 5, 1920.

" a. Recognition by the United States in October, 1915.

" b. Attacks on Americans by Villistas.

" c. Villa raid on Columbus, N. Mex., March, 1916.

" d. United States punitive expedition, March, 1916, to February, 1917.

" e. New Mexican Constitution put into effect on May 1, 1917.

" f. Presidential succession of 1920.

" g. Revolt in Sonora, spreading to all but three states, due to alleged partiality of Carranza in the electoral campaign.

" h. Flight and death of Carranza, May, 1920.

" 5 Huerta, interim president, May to November, 1920.

" a. Candidacy of General Obregon as constitutional president practically unopposed after withdrawal of the Carranza candidate.

" b. Efforts by the interim government to obtain recognition by the United States.

" c. Orderly elections of September, 1920, in which General Obregon receives an overwhelming vote for president."

A message from a Presbyterian pastor in Tabasco speaks of the tragedy of the war which threatened to arise between the United States and Mexico:

"Very dear Brethren in the Lord:

"I am sure that no true Christian in your nation desires war with Mexico, because such desires would be the denial of his Christian sentiments. May the thousands which make up our denomination in the United States express frankly and openly their attitude opposed to the terrible struggle, foreign to Christianity and civilization, and clearly against the culture of that great American people. Our Church should be the first to raise its Christian voice in authority against the savage struggle which may take both peoples no telling whither, covering them with desolation, ruin and ignominy, because the struggle would be terribly costly and long drawn out and one in which the blind fury of hate would let loose the most horrible deeds imaginable for the misfortune of both nations.

"Brethren, very beloved, it is urgent that you, in these moments, make your Christian influence felt so that the evil should not advance, but that on the contrary it may be clearly seen that the great spirit of Christ which abounds in you has dominated the blind passions of men. I beseech you to take into consideration my poor suggestions and to do all that you can in the way indicated. Would that we might soon see again tranquillity and peace extending themselves, so that our holy Christian cause

THE RED FLAG IN VERA CRUZ

This flag was hung out to show the tenants were on
rent strike (*p. 42*).

may advance with more vigor than ever before in this country that so much needs regeneration by Christ! May the Lord help you in your labors!

"Your affectionate brother in Christ."

The effect of the revolution on the fortunes of our Church and its members was indicated by letters received from the field. From the veteran pastor, Señor Arcadio Morales, pastor of the Presbyterian Church of *El Divino Salvador* in Mexico City, came this letter in 1914:

"The disembarking of the American troops in Vera Cruz; the most alarming rumors of their advance towards the capital of the republic; the proclamation of the Virgin of Guadalupe as the patron saint by the Minister of Public Instruction at a great public banquet; the appearing in one of the newspapers of the largest circulation, *El Imparcial,* of General Huerta pictured with this same Virgin, as the Priest Hidalgo is usually painted; the societies and corporations of all classes marching through the streets in manifestations hostile to the neighboring country and stoning everything that had the appearance of Yankee; the incendiary articles of the famous poet, Diaz Miron, who with fiery phrases invited the people to raid and destroy everything that had protection under the Stars and Stripes; the rabid propaganda carried on by the *Chapultepec, Vera Cruz,* and *Churubusco,* the yellowest of newspapers edited in the offices of the government, with the exclusive purpose of inflaming the patriotism of the people in favor of General Huerta and against the Americans; the zealous ef-

forts begun by the Roman clergy against the invasion, making use of the pulpit, the confessional,
the press, and all the numerous elements which they
could control in order to promote a Catholic rising
against those who did not support them — all this
produced a panic, an extraordinary excitement in
the capital.

"Everyone looked for the coming of a tremendous catastrophe; and we, the Protestants, so intimately related to the missionaries of the neighboring republic, felt that we were in greater danger
than anyone else, expecting every moment that
there would come down upon the Protestants a
furious persecution that would be another St.
Bartholomew's.

"Under such adverse circumstances the session
of *El Divino Salvador* Church had a meeting to
decide what we should do with the services, especially those in the wards, which surely could not
continue for lack of money to pay rents; and it was
certain that money would be lacking both from
outside and inside the country. But the session decided that the entire work should be carried on until
it was absolutely impossible to fulfill our mission to
proclaim the gospel of eternal salvation.

"And so we did. Day by day and night after
night, the doors of our church were always open
at the accustomed hours; with the exception of one
Sunday during the month of April when it seemed
wrong to expose the families by coming to church
on a night of dangers. With this one exception all
the congregations held their services regularly and

all the faithful and worthy helpers of the pastors were at their posts. There were times when the pastors had to urge the men not to come to the services on account of the conscription which truly desolated the capital, but in spite of all they did not fail to attend the divine services.

" We had, of course, to mourn the loss of twenty-three of the brethren who were conscripted in the army, there being one shot and three dying in battle, all the rest returning to their families, notwithstanding the fact that they were taken by land and sea to the farthest regions of the republic, but best of all was that while they were there they confessed Christ as their Saviour and worked for the heavenly Kingdom.

" It is probably not necessary to say that we have held our services at the places and times arranged for, but that we have received members, baptized children, remembered the death of our Lord in communion, performed marriages, held funeral services, and attended the meetings of the Christian Endeavor and Sunday school. We, of course, did not have to close any place of meeting for the lack of funds, for in spite of the great poverty of the church, all the missionary work of the city has been carried on. We had the pleasure of informing our brethren that the congregation of Lerdo, which for twenty-five years had been a paralytic that we had to carry in the arms of our faith, at last has entered into an era of such prosperity that frequently the meeting place is too small to accommodate the people who come to the services.

"Regarding the purpose of the Catholics of exterminating the Protestants, with the pretext of the American invasion and profanation of the most holy Virgin of Guadalupe, we can say that it failed completely, for not only were our places of meeting respected, as also our schools and our persons, but moreover we did not hear a single word of threat or insult from the inhabitants of the capital. We are convinced that the work which we have carried on in the pulpit, in the school, and in the press, disseminating the gospel truths for fifty years, has at last changed the opinion of the Mexican people, who have been convinced that the Protestants carry on a moral work, reforming the character of whatever person is near to us, and that all this about the ' Pacific Conquest' is a gross deceit.

"On account of the perilous circumstances which threatened the capital, the pastor had to change his residence to Tacuba. In order not to lose the connection which it was necessary for him to maintain with the congregations in the capital, he opened an office in Divino Salvador, discovering the confidence which the place inspires, as no less than one hundred people visited him there each month.

"We are convinced in this hour of security that the prayers of all our friends and brethren outside and inside the country have influenced greatly and to them we are also deeply grateful."

Some of our American missionaries did not escape threats and actual imprisonment. In 1914, Rev. N. J. Elliott was imprisoned for fifteen days in Saltillo, when he and his companions faced hardship and the daily threat of death. Mr. Elliott has put into writing the experiences of those days:

"A telegram flashed into Saltillo, Mexico, on April 21, 1914:

"Intervention is on. American Marines have landed in Vera Cruz. Give this publicity. — Huerta. Hang all Gringoes.' (It is believed that some operator added the last sentence.)

"The first I knew that anything serious had happened was that same afternoon when a policeman stepped up to me on the street and asked, 'Are you an American?' When I replied in the affirmative, he said, 'Come with me.' Little did I realize what was ahead of me. When we arrived at the military headquarters and were passing through the line of soldiers, I saw the American Consul entering just ahead of me. At that moment we knew he was a prisoner, too, and I felt there was little hope for our lives.

"We were taken into a rear room and searched. An armed guard was placed at the door. Some minutes later we heard the tramp of soldiers toward our door and another American was brought in. The guard at the door was doubled and the order given, 'Shoot any of those goats if they try to get out.' A fourth American was brought in and we were searched again. We were made to understand that we would be shot at midnight. We could hear the mobs yelling wildly in the streets outside, 'Death to the Gringoes!' As the town clock struck the midnight hour, we listened intently, but there was only the shuffling of the guards as they walked up and down. When the hour of one struck, we heard footsteps. An officer appeared and motioned for the Consul to follow. We waited anxiously for the volley. There was no sound and suddenly the officer appeared again and called for another one of us. Again we listened. When the officer appeared the third time, I was taken into the corridor; there I was again roughly searched. I saw the Consul and the other American between two rows of soldiers. I was placed in line also. The fourth American was brought out and placed behind me. Orders were given to march and we passed out into the street. A troop of cavalry fell in behind us.

"As we marched on toward the main street we waited for the order. Should the command be given, ' To the left! ' it meant the graveyard and only twenty minutes more of life; if ' To the right! ' the penitentiary was before us. Anxiously we waited the command. A heavy voice was heard above the rattling of the sabers and the clatter of the horses' hoofs, ' To the right! ' We breathed a sigh of relief. It was two o'clock in the morning. In the penitentiary were imprisoned some men who had lost their reason. We heard them in their cells on the first floor, howling and raving. The cells were built in tiers around an open court. We were put in cells on the fourth tier. We were anxious for the events of the morning for we knew that sunrise was a favorite hour for the shooting of prisoners. Our cells were dirty, foul-smelling, and alive with vermin. I fell into a brief sleep, only to

awaken chilled through, for we had neither bed nor
blankets. It was a hideous night. The guards
called their numbers roughly every fifteen minutes.
There were guards at the double cell-house door,
guards outside the cell house, guards on the roof,
guards in the outer court. Seven iron-barred doors
separated us from liberty. As daylight began to
appear, I waited once again for the footsteps of
the executioner. The morning wore on. No one
came to my cell. The jailer served food to the
Mexican prisoners, but neither food nor water
came my way. I thought I was to be left to die of
starvation and thirst. In the evening of the second
day, however, some prison food was brought to me
— coarse corn cake and ugly-smelling soup which
I could not eat. I learned from the guard that
there were eleven Americans in the prison, some
of them down on the first tier of cells. I found
that by directing my voice at just a certain angle
against the opposite wall I could talk with those
Americans on the first tier.

" On the third day of our imprisonment, a big
basket of food was sent to my cell with the card of
the British Consul of Saltillo. Those fried eggs
and that bread and pail of coffee brought tears to
my eyes. I sent the basket of food and coffee
around to the other American prisoners. Some
were afraid to eat it, fearing that poison had been
added after the food had reached the prison. In
the afternoon blankets were sent in to all through
the kindness of the British Consulate. ' You'll be
here for a day or two,' the guard would say, ' and

then you'll be sent to the wind.' At night we were told, ' Prepare to meet your God at sunrise!' The strain of close confinement and mental torture began to tell on us. The nights were hideous with the howling maniacs.

"We knew nothing of the international events taking place. If we had known the actual facts we should have been less hopeful. On the fifth day of our imprisonment the American Consul was ordered to give the combination to the Consulate safe. This looked bad for us, for the United States Government Code Book was to be taken. Thus the days wore on and no news came. We learned from the guard that there had been clashes between the United States marines and Mexican soldiers in Vera Cruz.

"As the Mexican rebel forces approached Saltillo an added danger faced us. If the rebels should attack the city, held by the Huerta federal forces who held us as prisoners, the federals would massacre us before retreating, and place the blame on the rebels. We learned of the mediation offer of Argentina, Brazil, and Chile, and that we were being held to see how it would terminate. On the fifth day the American Consul was taken before a military court and we had little hope for his life. In the afternoon of the same day we were taken before the same court and we thought that the mediation had failed between Mexico and the United States. We were asked to sign a document declaring that we had been imprisoned for our own protection and that we had been treated with all kindness. There was no hesitancy in signing such a document to get out of this place. We were allowed to go to the British Consulate under guard, where we were most kindly treated while we awaited the first train south to Mexico City. The British Vice Consul, H. J. Wheeler, had been tireless in his efforts to help us during our imprisonment. The train left two days later and we were taken as prisoners under guard to Mexico City and turned over to the Brazilian Ambassador who was in charge of the American Embassy, and who had worked for our release. We arrived in Mexico City, May 10. The Brazilian Ambassador urged me to remain in Mexico City and assist him in the Embassy, but I was anxious to see the United States again. The next day we went down to Vera Cruz. When we saw the American soldiers and marines in abundance on the streets and American battleships in the harbor, it was a sight to cheer a weary soul. When I saw 'Old Glory' waving from the flagstaff, I reverently took off my hat and thanked God that though I was not yet in my own land, I was safe under my own flag."

Some of our missionaries returned the first part of 1915 and gradually, as conditions became better, the full force entered upon the work there. The decisions in regard to the redistribution of territory were not fully carried out until after the conference held in 1919 in Mexico City. At a conference in the same city in 1917, agreements were made with reference to the organization of the Union

Theological Seminary, of a joint printing plant, paper, and depository, and of a local committee of coöperation. In 1917, the work at Saltillo and Aguascalientes was given up, Miss Wheeler, of Saltillo, going to take charge of the school at San Ángel, Miss Turner and Miss Spencer going to Vera Cruz, after spending a few months in Chiapas the preceding year.

Yucatan was occupied more fully in 1916, Dr. and Mrs. Molloy and Miss Bonine being sent there. The next year further reënforcements were added and a school for girls was opened at Mérida.

According to the original plan drawn up at Cincinnati the Presbyterian Church in the United States of America, or Northern Presbyterian Church, was to be responsible for the evangelization of the nine states and territories south of Mexico City, and was also to continue working in the Federal District in conjunction with the other Boards. A second conference was held in 1919 in Mexico City at which Dr. W. E. Browning was present. Here the decision was reached to turn over two of these states, Morelos and Guerrero, to the Presbyterian Church in the United States, the Southern Presbyterian Mission. Oaxaca was occupied as a station that year. Reënforcements were sent after that to Orizaba.

Such, in brief, was the development of the Mission to the year 1922, the year of the visitation of the Commission.

The present territory for which the Mission is responsible includes six states, one territory, and a

hare in the work in the Federal District. This
rea includes approximately one fifth of the popu-
ation and one fourth of the area of all Mexico.
The area and population of these states, accord-
ng to the census of 1910, with the comparison of
density of population with states in the United
States are as follows:

Name	Population 1910	Area sq. mi.	State with similar area in U. S.		Population per sq. mi.	State in U. S. with similar population per sq. mi.		Number of missionaries 1912
ampeche.........	86,685	18,089	Md.	12,327	4.7	Utah	4.5	3
hiapas...........	456,471	27,527	S. C.	30,989	16.1	Nebr.	15.5	..
ederal Dist.......	763,170	578	R. I.	1,248	1556.8	D. C.	5517.8	11
*axaca...........	1,059,789	35,689	Ind.	36,354	29.3	Ark.	30.	4
uintana Roo.....	9,328	19,274	W. Va.	24,170	.4	Nev.	.7	..
Vera Cruz.......	1,165,934	27,880	S. C.	30,989	38.7	La.	36.5	6
ucatan..........	347,781	15,939	Md.	12,327	9.6	N. Dak.	8.2	5
	3,889,158	144,976		148,404				29

Total population of Mexico (census of 1910), 15,150,369.
Average density of population in Mexico as a whole, 20 per square mile.
Average density of population in United States, 30 per square mile.
    *Presbyterian Board responsible for Southern two thirds of this State.

The growth and strength of the national Presbyterian Church since the revolution as indicated
in the Synod of Mexico, is described by two letters
from Rev. A. W. Wolfe, the first dated May
12, 1921:

" The Presbytery of Mexico City met a couple
of weeks ago. Plans were adopted and later approved by synod looking to the creation of a presbytery to include only the Federal District, another
in Oaxaca, another in Vera Cruz and Chiapas, and
another in the field occupied by the Southern Pres-

byterians. This last has already been formed
This reduction in the size will make possible more
frequent ' re-unions ' (a Spanishism for meeting)
and more efficient work on the part of the native
organization.

" The synod was an inspiring meeting. Every
presbytery and every congregation reported in
better condition than a year ago. The two sur-
prises came from the extremes. The *Presbiterio
Nacional Fronterizo,* composed of the congregations in the territory from which the Presbyterian Mission retired under the Cincinnati Plan
reported twenty-four organized churches and
twenty-nine congregations, fourteen ministers,
three licentiates, three students preaching, seven
school-teachers studying in the Presbytery's seminary in Saltillo, 2,956 members (half the total
number of Presbyterians in Mexico), and $44,000
(pesos) raised. The *Presbiterio del Golfo,* comprising Yucatan, Campeche, and Tabasco, met and
reorganized after seven years, ordained a couple
of men, licensed three more, and reported $40,000
(pesos) raised by the congregations, there being quite a number of self-supporting congregations."

The second letter, dated July 12, 1922, was as
follows:

" I am just back from a splendid meeting of
synod.

" Cohesion and unanimity were manifest among
all the branches of our widely scattered Church.
The self-sustaining presbytery was the only one

AN OATH TO BE TRUE TO THE PROTESTANT FAITH

Sworn in memory of a leader who had been killed
by Roman Catholics (*p. 49*).

which presented complete reports. As nearly as could be determined some 1,200 members were received in the past year, giving a present membership of about 9,000 (the same as the Methodist). The churches raised about $120,000 (pesos). There are some forty ministers and as many candidates.

"The synod is the only native body in Mexico that takes the initiative in evangelistic plans. They followed the lead of the United States of America Church and reduced the standing committees to four. They voted to celebrate the twenty-fifth anniversary of the synod in 1926 by the organization of a General Assembly with three synods. In that year they hope to break ground for a $400,000 (pesos) cathedral church in Mexico City. They will ask the two Presbyterian Boards to contribute toward this fund, but expect to raise most of it themselves. All existing churches are to be self-sustaining by that time.

"The present year is to see a church-wide evangelistic campaign directed by a strong committee, which will extend over the entire year. The goal is set for 2,000 new professions of faith. By 1926 we expect to have 15,000 members at the very least.

"Following the synod meeting we went to Toluca to attend the great National Convention of Sunday Schools, Young People's Societies, and Christian Workers. The Presbyterian church of Toluca seats 600, but over 800 attended some sessions. More than 400 delegates were registered. A large chorus from Coyoacán and San Ángel,

directed by Mr. Brown, sang repeatedly, making
a fine impression."

At one of the Jubilee sessions of the Presbyte
rian Mission and Church, held in November, 1922
to commemorate the fifty years of Presbyteria
work in Mexico, Rev. P. Arellano,[1] one of the lead
ing national pastors, spoke with feeling and witl
marked effect of those who had given their live
to the service of the Church. His address is
fitting recapitulation of the progress of the pas
fifty years of the Presbyterian Church in Mexic
and of the part played by both American and Mex
ican leaders, under God's guidance, in bringing
the Mission and Church to their present stage o
development:

" In our National Day we remember with lov
and gratitude the heroes who fought and gave thei
lives that we might have country and nationality
It is altogether fitting, therefore, that the Presby
terian Church in celebrating its Jubilee year shoul
remember, inspired by spiritual love, those wh
took the first steps in the struggles of bringing ou
faith to a waiting people. Some of them seale
their testimony with the blood of their earthly life
and all of them offered up on the altar of servic
the best of their lives. Let us here, before th
graves that hold their remains, bow in respect t
their devotion.

" In remembering the names of these self-sacri
ficing men we include instinctively the nationals a

[1] Dr. Arellano died on October 5, 1923. His name should b
enrolled in the list of those who rendered conspicuous service t
the Church in Mexico.

well as the foreigners: the former, because by blood they are ours; the latter, because they gave themselves to the evangelization of Mexico and thereby they belong to us and we ourselves glory in their work.

"I wish to mention first the career of Rev. Abraham Gomez, one of the first and most intellectual of our workers who paid the full measure of his devotion to the cause of God at the hands of assassins. Born of an Indian family in a small village of the state of Mexico, he began his preparation for the ministry in the schools of our Church. He was ordained a preacher in 1885 and held the pastorate of different churches. While he was the pastor at Aguacatlitlan he was killed, on August 7, 1887. He was only twenty-one years old when the intolerance of fanaticism smote him to death.

"Recalling another of our national workers, I wish to mention the name of Procopio G. Diaz, who, traveling through dangerous districts to initiate the work of our Church in various parts of the Republic, suffered and bore upon his body the marks of martyrdom. He was born in 1828, in Tixtla. Left an orphan in his twelfth year, he provided himself with the most elementary sort of education. For a time he became a weaver and later a printer; and took great advantage of his habit of reading, which enabled him to excell in his study of the law. He entered, as a private soldier, one of the revolutionary armies, and during the War of Intervention he was given the com-

mission of a colonel. Converted in 1874, he began
to work for the establishment of a Christian church
in Acapulco, and, in coöperation with Mr. N. N.
Hutchinson, arranged the plans with great rejoic-
ing until the fatal night in which he was the victim
of a vicious wound upon his forehead with a for-
midable machete. Later he was obliged to leave
his post, together with other coworkers. Consecrated as he was to the work, he had a large share
in the establishment of the church in Chilpancingo.
When he joined the Presbyterian Mission he
brought with him his printing shop and with it he
laid the foundations of the publishing house of
our Church. He wrote various pamphlets and
collaborated in the publishing of the hymnal. For
twenty years he served as the initiator of the work
of God in various parts of our country and also
as a consistent preacher of the Word of repentance.

" We must speak of the work of Dr. J. Milton
Greene, one of our great missionaries, who accomplished great things for the Kingdom of God.
He was born in 1842, in the state of New York
Through the influence of his uncle, a pastor, he
became interested in the ministry, and with the
assistance of his uncle, he attended Princeton University. Graduated from the college of this in
stitution he remained in the school of theology
until December, 1866. After he had served a
pastor of various churches in his own country for
period of nearly fifteen years, he was sent t
Mexico as a missionary in 1881. In 1882 h
founded the *Escuela Normal Presbiteriana*. O

account of ill health he returned to his native country and there served as pastor for some time. Later he again entered missionary work at Porto Rico and later in Cuba, where he completed a period of fifty years of service in the work of God. After a most consistent and brilliant missionary work he was permitted to retire in his seventy-ninth year. Those of us who had the privilege of knowing him will always remember him as the man who inspired others with the strength of his Christian character and with his kindly attitude towards his fellow men everywhere.

"We remember Dr. Hubert W. Brown as the team mate and successor of Dr. Greene. Dr. Brown was born in the state of Ohio in 1858. He attended the University of Michigan, receiving there his degrees of A.B. and A.M. He attended the Theological School of Princeton University, and shortly after he had left there he was sent to Mexico as a missionary and assistant to Dr. Greene. His great zeal and his contact with Dr. Greene enabled him to identify himself with the Mexicans as their friend and coworker. His interest in the spiritual welfare of his own countrymen residing in Mexico led him to the establishment of the Union Church. His great energy and his wide intellectual resourcefulness gave him a very large field of activities. He was the treasurer of the Mission, preacher, teacher, editor, and author. After a strenuous service of twenty years he died at the age of forty-eight.

" Dr. Arcadio Morales was the first native worker

in our Church. The first minister, he was also the first in the service of almost all the departments of our Church's work in Mexico. He was born in 1849 in the City of Mexico. In his days of childhood and young manhood he was given very little, if any, opportunity of education. While he was at his work as a master weaver, he received the first inspiration of the gospel. After a time of religious experience with the Episcopal Church he organized the first Presbyterian church in Mexico in 1872. He conducted the services at this church and later dedicated all his life activity to the ministry. He helped to carry on the work in the very earnestness of his heart. He was identified with every phase of the evangelical activities of Mexico, so much so that he was later called the ' Moody of Mexico.' Our National Church may well feel proud of his work, and may the gracious God grant us men of the type of Dr. Morales that His own work in Mexico may prosper.

" We remember with gratitude the name of Mr. N. N. Hutchinson, a man of aristocratic bearing yet accessible to all. There was no difficulty great enough to prevent him from doing that which was asked of him by the people among whom he was a missionary. He served his God both personally and with his money, for with his own means he purchased the only two places of worship that our Church owns in Mexico City. He was one of the first to be interested in the organization of classes where prospective ministers might be trained.

" But there are many others in the list of our

missionaries and workers, whose part in the early establishment of our Church was as important as that of those already mentioned. These names carry with them the inspiration that comes with the expressed desire of regeneration. May I not now mention their names: Dr. Thomas F. Wallace, Brigido Sepulveda, Gregorio García, Josué Martinez, Luís Amaya, Pedro M. Rodríguez, Hipolito Quezada, Clemente Salazar, Benjamin Pascal, Manuel Zavaleta, Hesiquio Forncada, Daniel Rodríguez, Dr. Juan Moya, Enrique Blanchi, Leopoldo M. Diaz, Felipe Pastrana, J. P. Nevarez, Felix Gomez, Miguel Arias, Luís Arias, Levi Andres Perez, Maximo Palomino Emilio Torres, Julian Mesa. Many of these died in the service of the Lord. All of them consecrated the best part of their lives, and we here mention their names with love and gratitude. Let us in devotion to their consecration place this flower upon their tombs."

REMAKING THE MISSIONARY MAP OF MEXICO

THE outstanding events in the history of the last decade in Mexico have been, in the political world, the revolution, and in the Church, the inception, adoption, and development of the so-called Cincinnati Plan.

When, in 1914, at the suggestion of President Wilson, owing to the disturbed condition of the country and the occupation of Vera Cruz by the American forces, a large number of missionaries were withdrawn from Mexico, it was proposed that a convention of missionary forces at work in Mexico should be held for the purpose of considering the problems that concerned all societies and of discovering, if possible, a more effective way to carry on the work in Mexico.

The different Churches had, as in other countries, opened work in many different parts of the land without taking into consideration the fact that other communions were working in the same places.

Our own Mission and Church work was greatly overextended. We had work in fifteen states or districts. The other Missions were also scattered but not quite so widely.

The distribution was not even. Certain more advanced states had in them three or four Missions and a disproportionate number of schools, while others were occupied only in name, especially some of the southern states where we had one or two Mexican ministers. In some states there was one missionary to each twelve thousand people, in others scarcely one to over a million. Fourteen of the states, with a population of over five millions, or one third of the entire population, had no resident foreign missionaries. There were thirty-nine mission high schools in fifteen states, while in the other fifteen states and territories there were no schools.

The proposed convention was held in Cincinnati on June 30 and July 1, 1914. It was attended by representatives of the Northern Baptists, Methodists, Northern and Southern, Presbyterians, Northern and Southern, Friends, Disciples of Christ, Congregationalists, Episcopalians, the Young Men's Christian Association, and the American Bible Society.

Great unanimity of view and spirit prevailed, and a very distinct step in advance was taken. The convention agreed upon united effort in publication and press work and in theological education, adopted certain principles for the development of educational institutions, and agreed upon the principle of division of territory. The report of the Committee on Territorial Occupation, which was adopted, included the following statements:

" 1. The Committee is deeply impressed with the inadequacy of the missionary force available for the evangelistic, educational, and other forms

of missionary effort through which we are seeking
to help Mexico. There is an average of one foreign
missionary or missionary's wife to 70,000 of the
population. Fourteen of the states of Mexico,
with a population of over 5,000,000, or one third
of the entire population, have no resident foreign
missionaries.

" 2. The Committee believes that there should be
a great increase of the missionary staff to coöperate
with the loyal and capable ministers of the Mexican
churches, and that as soon as possible the force of
missionaries should be increased at least fifty per
cent.

" 3. The Committee believes also that there
might be a more effective distribution of the present
missionary forces than that which has come about
in the natural development of the work hitherto.
In some states there is one missionary to each 12,000
people and in others there is not one to more than
1,000,000. There are thirty-nine mission high
schools in fifteen states, while the other fifteen
states, with a population of 6,000,000, have no such
institutions at work for their people. We would
accordingly urge upon each agency at work in
Mexico the earnest consideration of the location
and distribution of its forces, so as to avoid duplication and overlapping and to secure the occupation and evangelization of the entire field.

" 4. It is not within the province or power of
the Committee to indicate any withdrawals or
transfers which might be made by particular agencies, and we recognize that there are denominations

which do not feel free to share in any plan of territorial assignment of responsibility; but we recommend that in the development of the work in Mexico and in the effort to provide for the occupation of the whole country the following denominations be regarded by this Conference as primarily responsible for the occupation and missionary cultivation of the states indicated."

Then followed the list of Boards with the assignments agreed upon. It was further agreed that:

" In such states as Tamaulipas, in municipalities of 10,000 people or less, where more than one Board is at work, all are to withdraw with the exception of one Board, priority of occupation to be given first consideration.

" In municipalities of 20,000 people, when occupied by more than two Boards, all are to withdraw with the exception of two, priority of occupation to be given first consideration.

" In all new territory assigned to a single Board, all other Boards are to refrain from entering."

The plan proposed for division of territory at this first conference was not final, as there were various adjustments and changes approved at subsequent conferences in 1917 and 1919. But the principles of coöperation, and of avoidance, whenever possible, of duplication of effort, have been accepted and put into general effect.

Our Presbyterian Mission was to withdraw from Nuevo León, Coahuila, San Luis Potosí, Aguascalientes, and Zacatecas, and to develop its work in the south, taking over the work in Oaxaca and

Vera Cruz from the Methodist Episcopal Church.

The official action of the Presbyterian Board on October 6, 1914, was as follows:

" The Mexico Committee reported that it had considered carefully the report of the Cincinnati Conference of the missionaries working in Mexico, representing the various Boards of the different denominations, and the recommendations therein contained covering such matters as division of territory, union in educational and theological work, and the uniting of the work of the various presses. They have offered the following report which was adopted:

" ' On June 30 and July 1 there was held in the city of Cincinnati, Ohio, a Conference on Missions in Mexico. This Conference was called by the Latin American Committee of the Foreign Missions Conference. It was attended by some sixty delegates, secretaries, officers, and furloughed missionaries representing eleven Boards and Societies carrying on evangelistic work in Mexico. Five of our missionaries and two members of the Executive Staff, Secretary Speer, who for many years had the correspondence with the Mexican Mission, and Secretary Halsey, with whose office the correspondence is now being carried on, were present.

" ' The object of the Conference was to discuss the best ways and means of reëstablishing the work in Mexico on a broad union basis when, in the providence of God, conditions in the republic should warrant the return to Mexico of the missionaries. Most careful preparation had been

REV. JOSÉ COFFIN
Leader of the churches in Chiapas (*p. 47*).

DR. ARCADIO MORALES
Pastor in Mexico City for fifty-three years (*p. 79*).

MEXICAN PROTESTANT LEADERS OF THE PAST AND PRESENT GENERATIONS

made for the Conference; a series of papers giving full data regarding the work of all missionary organizations engaged in evangelistic and educational efforts in the republic was prepared and distributed to the delegates before the opening of the Conference. The deliberations of the Conference, lasting two days and one evening, were marked by a spirit of unity, harmony, and missionary fervor rarely witnessed, and the conclusions reached were practically unanimous.

" ' With the exception of one or two Boards or Societies, practically all the evangelical agencies in Mexico were represented at the Conference. As soon as the typewritten copies of the report of the Conference were received, about the middle of July, the full minutes were sent to each member of the Committee on Mexico with a note from the secretary asking that the whole matter be carefully considered and reported on at the first meeting in September. The full report of the Conference has since been printed and a copy is now in the hands of each member of the Board. Your Committee has given this whole subject careful consideration, and in presenting the report of this Cincinnati Conference on Mexico, as it does to-day, would express warm appreciation of the purposes and ideals of this Conference and of the spirit of sacrifice shown by our representatives in their willingness to relinquish work which had become dear by long association, in order that a more efficient service might be rendered by the entire Church to the needy people of the Republic of Mexico.

" ' 1. Your Committee would call attention to
the fact that many of the recommendations herein
made are only such as the Board has already car
ried out in other fields and with the approval of the
General Assembly, and in line with that spirit of
unity which has characterized the work of the
Board during all its history.

" ' It is proposed to call the Church in Mexico
by the name of " The Evangelical Church in Mex
ico." In Spanish this is the exact equivalent of
the name of the Church in the Philippines. It is
proposed to unite all the various presses and publi
cation agencies, and the Sunday-school papers and
literature. The Board for years has been endeavor
ing to bring about this result in connection with
the press and publishing work of the Methodist
Episcopal Church. The proposed union in theo
logical education is one which has long been be
fore the minds of the Mexican missionaries because
of the small number of candidates now attending
the seminary and the splendid equipment which
the Board possesses, which could easily be utilized
by all the Boards. The various educational changes
suggested are along the line which the Board is
vigorously prosecuting in other missions, and some
of the other changes now recommended by the
Cincinnati Conference have long been thought of by
representatives of your own Board. Anyone who
knows Mexico cannot question for a moment that
the one thing she needs above all else is Christian
education, and the plans here outlined by the Con
ference, which the Board is asked to adopt, are, in

the judgment of your Committee, admirably adapted to the present and future needs of the Mexican Republic. We recommend that the Board approve the resolutions on education, leaving it to the Executive Council to work out the details in particular cases, and when satisfactory arrangements have been made with other Boards, to report the same for action to the Board.

" ' 2. Your Committee would call special attention to the resolutions adopted on territorial occupation. This Committee was the largest in the entire Conference; its deliberations were carried on far into the night and its conclusions were reached only after much discussion, much prayer, and much yielding of valuable property on the part of many of the Boards represented including your own. While it is true that your Board relinquishes under the proposed agreement valuable schools such as those of Saltillo and Aguascalientes and work in several of the important stations in north and central Mexico, yet it has had assigned to it a large, fruitful, and, in many cases, virgin territory. [The field in Mexico assigned to the Northern Presbyterian Church for its evangelization is made up of the states of Yucatan, Campeche, Tabasco, Chiapas, Vera Cruz, Oaxaca, Guerrero, and Morelos, for which we are to have the sole responsibility, and in addition the state of Mexico and the Federal District where we are to share the responsibility with the Methodist Episcopal Church and the Baptists.]

" ' While there are many difficulties to be overcome, many readjustments to be made, much new land to be possessed, and many problems arising out of this change of location, yet we believe that this assignment opens to the Board a magnificent opportunity for splendid service such as it has never rendered before in Mexico, and that it helps to make possible the movement which is fraught with the choicest consequences for good in the entire land.

" ' In regard to the recommendations, your Committee would advise that they be referred to the Executive Council with power, the Board giving its general consent to the proposals, as indicated in the resolutions, leaving it to the Council to work out the full details and report as they may be satisfactorily adjusted with the other Boards and Societies doing work in Mexico. To give some idea of the changes that are involved in the new territorial divisions, one of the best informed missionaries suggested that we would need to establish Stations for resident missionaries as follows:

STATION	FIELD
1. Coyoacán — San Ángel	Mexico State and Federal District
2. Cuernavaca — Iguala	States of Morelos and Guerrero
3. Orizaba — Jalapa	State of Vera Cruz
4. Oaxaca	State of Oaxaca
5. Tuxtla Gutiérrez or San Cristóbal	State of Chiapas and part of Oaxaca
6. Mérida or San Juan Bautista or some point on the Isthmus of Tehuantepec	States of Yucatan, Campeche, and Tabasco

" ' 3. That the Board approve the series of general resolutions adopted by the Conference and express its willingness to coöperate with other Boards and Societies represented in the Conference in the uniting of the various agencies in Mexico for the purpose of greater efficiency.

" ' 4. Your Committee notes the request of a number of the Mexican missionaries now home on furlough that there should be a conference with the missionaries and the Executive Council to discuss these various problems arising out of the new policies suggested by the Cincinnati Conference. Your Committee recommends that the Executive Council call such a conference, at New York or at some other city, or at some convenient place, where the members of the Executive Council and the missionaries can arrange with greater minuteness the various details connected with the changes made necessary by the above actions of the Board.

" ' In adopting this new policy, which means progress and efficiency and larger things for the Kingdom, the Board should recognize that it involves the sending of a much larger number of missionaries and an increased expenditure of money.

" ' At present the Board has but eight men at work in Mexico, only three of these being devoted exclusively to evangelistic work. The total number of missionaries in Mexico under our Board at present is nineteen. Under the new arrangement in the very near future at least sixty workers would be required adequately to man the new work as planned in the above resolution.

" ' Recent letters received from missionaries in

Texas and from other representatives of the native
Church on the field indicate that Mexican hearts
and minds are more open to the gospel to-day than
ever before in all the long history of Mexican mis
sions, and that there is a correspondingly strong
appeal to the American Church to meet this need.' "

Years passed before the remaining details of this
division could be worked out. In a regional conference held in Mexico City on March 31, 1917
an agreement was reached by representatives of
the Methodist Churches North and South, both
branches of the Presbyterian Church, Congregational, Associate Reformed Presbyterian Church
Friends, and Disciples. The readjustment adopted
at this conference concerned the states in the North
The Northern Baptists, who had decided to throw
in their lot with the Southern Baptists, withdrew
from the coöperative agreement and the division
was adjusted between the Methodist Episcopal
Church, South, Disciples, and Congregationalists
The Protestant Episcopal Church had also declined
to enter into the coöperative agreement. The Presbyterian Church of the United States was to withdraw from Nuevo León and Tamaulipas.

This plan was not formally approved by the
Boards concerned until two years later, when it was
incorporated, with some changes, in the plan of
division adopted by the conference in Mexico in
February, 1919.

The principal changes included in this final plan
were the withdrawal of the Methodist Episcopal
Church from Sinaloa, Jalisco, and Colima in favor

f the Congregationalists, who in turn withdrew
rom their original assignment in northern Sonora
nd Chihuahua to make room for the Methodist
Episcopal Church, South, and the Methodist Epis-
opal Church yielded Michoacán which had been
ssigned to them in the original plan, to make room
or the Presbyterians of the United States. The
atter left their former fields in the states of Ta-
naulipas, Nuevo León, and San Luis Potosí, and
ook up the field, east of Mexico City, of Michoa-
án, from the Methodist Episcopal Church and of
Mexico (in part), Morelos, and Guerrero, from our
riginal assignment.

The plan as now adopted gives to the Methodist
Episcopal Church, South, the entire border line
with the exception of Matamoros; to the Congregational Mission, the west coast as far south as the
ine of Mexico City; to the Disciples and Methodist
Episcopal Church, compact central fields on the
able-land; and to the Presbyterian Churches of the
United States and the United States of America
ll the southern end of the republic. A comparison
f the location and assignments of the various Mis-
ions in 1913, before the Cincinnati Conference,
with their assignments in 1919, after the final con-
erence in Mexico City, is given at the close of this
chapter. A map showing the revised allocation is
given on the opposite page.

In the early discussions of the plan by the Presbyterian Mission, the suggestion was made that the
boys' school at Coyoacán should be moved to Oaxaca, but later this proposal was dropped. It was

proposed also that a girls' school should be opened
in Chiapas or Oaxaca. This school eventually
opened in Vera Cruz.

In a letter to Dr. Halsey, April 8, 1919, which
took up among other things this whole question
Mr. Petran wrote:

" The differences of opinion in working out the
Cincinnati Plan . . . are now all settled. It may
seem that it took a long time to settle them, but
when the disturbed condition of the country is taken
into consideration, and the fact that it was found
necessary to make changes in the assignments of
most Missions, it can be felt now that the final ad
justments, after most ample discussion, will have
the largest possible acceptance."

The division of territory in Mexico City and the
Federal District has worked out in 1922, with the
exception of one suburb where negotiations were in
progress when the congregation, somewhat impa
tient at the slowness of the Ecclesiastical Com
mittee in deciding their fate, decided to form a
union church.

The plan regarding division of territory as now
in practice, is, with one or two exceptions, working
well between the Missions. The fields are now com
pact. While our Presbyterian Mission has given
up well-established work in the five centers men
tioned above, other churches have surrendered much
in the interest of the greater efficiency of this plan

When our Presbyterian Mission entered upon
the new program, it possessed property in the Fed
eral District, in Jalapa, and in Vera Cruz. It had

o permanent equipment at all in the states of
Oaxaca, Tabasco, Chiapas, Campeche, Yucatan
except church property in Mérida), and the ter-
itory of Quintana Roo. Subsequently property
vas transferred from the Methodist Mission and
Board in the city of Oaxaca in the state of Oaxaca
nd in the city of Orizaba in the state of Vera Cruz.
Additional property has been secured in Jalapa,
o replace the property destroyed by the earthquake
1 1920.

Commenting further upon the shift from the
orthern to the southern part of Mexico, Dr. W.
C. Browning stated in his report, after his visit to
he field in 1919:

" The trip north also convinced me, if I needed
onviction, that the Presbyterian Board has gone
he second mile, if not the third and fourth, in its
acrifice of established work in the interests of co-
peration. Schools and organized churches, the re-
ult of many years of consecrated labor, have been
acrificed willingly to the common good, and prop-
rties will be turned over, generally at a loss, in
pite of generous impulses that may develop on the
art of our successors."

In the Kingdom he who loses his life gains it,
nd this law is true of those who gave up, for the
ake of the Kingdom, fields long occupied and much
ved. The larger field of opportunity, though
endered less fruitful by the backwardness of the
eople and the ignorance and superstition of their
earts, is nevertheless " the open door set before
s." The Presbyterian Mission and Board, which,

through their leaders, Dr. Speer and Dr. Halsey, had the honor of proposing this plan, have also the honor of making one of the largest sacrifices in withdrawal, as well as the opportunity of inheriting perhaps the most difficult field in the republic.

PROTESTANT MISSIONS IN MEXICO
OLD AND NEW PLANS

Distribution by Societies in 1913 and the Readjustments Resulting from the Cincinnati Conference of 1914, and the Conferences in Mexico City in 1917 and 1919.

NOTE: The Baptist (North and South) and Episcopal Boards did not see their way clear to join in the coöperative allocations agreed upon. Where two or more Boards are located in one state, under the revised plan different sections of the state are assigned to each society.

State and Pop. (1910)	Station	Societies at Work	Revised Location
1. Aguascalientes (124,447)	Aguascalientes Aguascalientes	Baptist (N.) Presbyterian (N)	Disciples
2. Campeche (86,685)	None	None	Presbyterian
3. Chiapas (456,371)	Tuxtla	Baptist (N.)	Presbyterian (N.)
4. Chihuahua (423,387)	Chihuahua Chihuahua Chihuahua Chihuahua Juares Sta. Rosalia Parral	Congregational Methodist (S.) Episcopal Baptist (S.) Baptist (S.) Baptist (S.) Congregational	Methodist (S.)
5. Coahuila (376,747)	Piedras Negras Sabinas Sabinas Saltillo Saltillo Saltillo Saltillo Torreón Torreón Torreón	Disciples Disciples Baptist (N.) Baptist (S.) Disciples Methodist (S.) Presbyterian (N.) Baptist (S.) Methodist (S.) Episcopal	Methodist (S.)

ate and Pop. (1910)	*Station*	*Societies at Work*	*Revised Location*
3. Colima (80,500)	None	None	Congregational
7. Durango (509,585)	Durango Durango	Baptist (S.) Methodist (S.)	Methodist (S.)
8. Guanajuato (1,085,681)	Guanajuato León	Methodist (N.) Baptist (S.)	Methodist (N.)
9. Guerrero (620,416)	Chilpancingo Chilpancingo	Presbyterian (N.) Episcopal	Presbyterian (S.)
9. Hidalgo (655,187)	Tula Pachuca	Methodist (S.) Methodist (N.)	Methodist (N.)
1. Jalisco (1,220,160)	Guadalajara Guadalajara Guadalajara Guadalajara Guadalajara	Methodist (S.) Adventist Congregational Baptist (S.) Episcopal	Congregational
2. Lower California (53,254)	None	None	Congregational
3. Mexico (1,000,903)	Toluca Toluca	Baptist (S.) Episcopal	Presbyterian (S.) Methodist (N.)
4. Federal Dist. (763,170)	Mexico City Mexico City Mexico City Mexico City Mexico City Mexico City	Baptist (N.) Adventist Methodist (N.) Methodist (S.) Presbyterian (N.) Episcopal	Methodist (N.) Methodist (S.) Presbyterian (N.)
. Michoacán (1,003,491)	Morelia Zitácuaro	Baptist (S.) Presbyterian (N.)	Presbyterian (S.)
3. Morelos (183,705)	Morelos (?)	Episcopal	Presbyterian (S.) Methodist (N.)
. Nayarit (175,731)	None	None	Congregational
3. Nuevo León (373,207)	Monterey Monterey Monterey Monterey Monterey Linares Linares Monte Morelos	Baptist (N.) Adventist Disciples Methodist (S.) Episcopal Presbyterian (S.) Baptist (N.) Presbyterian (S.)	Methodist (S.) Friends

State and Pop. (1910)	Station	Societies at Work	Revised Location
19. Oaxaca (1,059,789)	Oaxaca	Baptist (N.)	Presbyterian (N.)
	Oaxaca	Episcopal	
	Oaxaca	Methodist (N.)	
20. Puebla (1,118,439)	Puebla	Methodist (N.)	Methodist (N.)
	Puebla	Baptist (N.)	
	Puebla	Episcopal	
21. Querétaro (247,195)	Querétaro	Methodist (N.)	Methodist (N.)
22. Quintana Roo (9,328)	None	Presbyterian (N.)	Presbyterian (N.)
23. S. Luis Potosí (638,832)	S. L. Potosí	Methodist (S.)	Disciples
	S. L. Potosí	Adventist	Associate Reformed
	S. L. Potosí	Baptist (N.)	Presbyterian
	S. L. Potosí	Presbyterian (N.)	Friends
	Matehuala	Friends	
24. Sinaloa (329,317)	Mazatlán	Methodist (S.)	Congregational
25. Sonora (275,107)	Guaymas	Baptist (S.)	Congregational
	Guaymas	Methodist (S.)	Methodist (S.)
	Hermosillo	Congregational	
	Nacozari	Episcopal	
26. Tabasco (193,675)	None	None	Presbyterian (N.)
27. Tamaulipas (256,278)	Matamoros	Presbyterian (S.)	Methodist (S.)
	Matamoros	Friends	Friends
	Victoria	Friends	Associate Reformed
	Victoria	Presbyterian (S.)	Presbyterian
	Tampico	Episcopal	
	Tampico	Baptist (N.)	
28. Tlaxcala (183,000)	Tlaxcala	Methodist (N.)	Methodist (N.)
29. Vera Cruz (1,165,934)	Jalapa	Presbyterian (N.)	Presbyterian (N.)
	Jalapa	Episcopal	Associate Reformed
	Orizaba	Methodist (N.)	Presbyterian
30. Yucatan (347,781)	Mindo	Presbyterian (N.)	Presbyterian (N.)
31. Zacatecas (480,690)	Zacatecas	Presbyterian (N.)	Disciples

JAMES B. RODGEF

MAP OF MEXICO WITH COOPERATIVE DIVISION OF TERRITORY
CONFERENCE OF 1914, AND CON

MAP
OF
MEXICO

Showing Division of Responsibility for Occupation of Territory by Missionary Societies as Agreed Upon at the Conference of Christian Workers, City of Mexico, February 15-21, 1919

The program of co-operation adopted includes:

A University in the City of Mexico,

A Hospital in the City of Mexico,

Eight Agricultural Schools in as many different centers of the Republic;

A School of Mechanical Arts in each important center,

Normal Schools in such districts as do not yet possess them, and the strengthening of those already existing;

Development of the Union Theological Seminary already existing in Mexico City;

A Community Center or Institutional Church in each important center in the Republic;

A Union Publishing House, Union Paper, and Book Store, in City of Mexico;

A Campaign to popularize Medical Knowledge;

Definite division of territorial responsibility so as to avoid overlapping or duplication of effort.

KEY TO AREAS AND APPROXIMATE POPULATION OF EACH

Congregational 1,880,000

Methodist Episcopal, South 1,610,000

Friends 285,000

Disciples of Christ 1,005,000

Associate Reformed Presby. 550,000

Methodist Episcopal 3,900,000

Presbyterian (South) 2,125,000

Presbyterian (North) 3,050,000

MILES 100 50 0 100 200

CHAPTER XV

PROGRESS AND PROBLEMS IN PROTESTANT COÖPERATION

1. The Institutions Developed Under the Cincinnati Plan

THE first section of this chapter deals with the union and coöperative institutions established since the Cincinnati Plan was approved and with certain problems in Church relationships which have arisen in northern Mexico subsequent to 1914.

Following the adoption of the general principles of the Cincinnati Plan, certain union institutions of importance have been developed in Mexico. These include a union theological seminary, a union press and periodical, and a union hospital. Plans for a union university and for union in the schools have not as yet been carried out in detail. Coöperation in temperance work has been successfully accomplished.

After the Cincinnati Conference, the Northern Baptist Mission decided to unite forces with their brethren of the Baptist Church South, both in forming associations and in the establishment of a seminary. Their Seminary occupies the building of the former *Escuela Normal* in Saltillo, which at present, and until they can finish the building of their own seminary plant, they are renting from us.

The Baptist churches are scattered all over the land and it is to be regretted that they have not seen their way to unite more closely with us. There is this to be said, however, in regard to their Seminary — that Mexico is a very large country and that there are serious difficulties, first in securing men to go from the North to Mexico City for theological education, and second, in having them go back after they are educated. Some have even thought that it would be wise to have students from other Churches besides the Baptists unite with them in study in the North.

The Presbyterian pastor at Saltillo, Coahuila, has asked the Mission and the Board to grant to the Frontier Presbytery the use of the building at Saltillo, when the Baptists give it up, in order that they may start a seminary of their own. At other times they spoke of having a girls' school in this building for the benefit of the Presbyterian churches of the North. As yet the Mission has not approved of granting this petition, especially because the Methodist Episcopal Church, South, has an excellent school in Saltillo, and the Mission feels that our Seminary in Mexico is for the present sufficient for our needs.

We found that perhaps too large a proportion of the work of the Seminary in Mexico City was piled on the shoulders of Dr. Howland and Dr. Wallace, as the Methodists have been unable to find a man who could give his entire time to the Seminary this past year. This, of course, is only an incident in the career of the Seminary. Mr.

Christian spirit has been shown by the physicians in charge. Our Board should coöperate in some measure in this hospital and should also look forward to the union hospital needed in Mexico City.

The Executive Secretary of the Regional Committee on Coöperation in Mexico is partially supported by funds contributed by denominational Temperance Boards in the United States, and is giving a part of his time to the promotion of this great cause. The president of the republic, General Obregon, and other leaders, are greatly interested in this movement and the prediction is freely made that within a comparatively short time Mexico will imitate the example given by the United States in the adoption of an amendment prohibiting the sale of intoxicating beverages. Two states have already adopted " dry " legislation, and there is a widespread sentiment throughout the republic in favor of prohibition.

It is fortunate that the evangelical Missions of the country can take a leading part in this movement, through their Regional Committee on Coöperation, and the Boards which are contributing to this work, including our own, may feel that the expenditure is justified.

Mexico, as no other country in the world, represents the triumph of coöperative Christian work over that of the old-line, sectarian program, and the whole Church gains thereby.

2. The Attitude of the Native Church in the North Toward the Cincinnati Plan

Although in general throughout Mexico the native churches have coöperated in putting into effect the Cincinnati Plan, as modified in the Conferences in 1917 and 1919, special problems have arisen with reference to the independent Presbyterian churches in the North, following the withdrawal of our missionaries from that territory. The printed report of the Cincinnati Conference concludes with the following statement:

" It was recognized by all that it was indispensable that the plans should have the approval and support of the leaders, both men and women, in the Mexican churches, and the representatives of each Board were requested not only to lay the report of the Conference before their own Boards and their own home churches, but also to take up the various questions involved with the Mexican churches."

Dr. Speer's letter of July 21, 1914, urged the Mission to present the matter to the Mexican leaders. On July 31, 1914, Dr. Halsey wrote to the Mexican missionaries, in part, as follows:

" I am writing this letter for certain specific reasons: First, if any of the missionaries have any comments to make on the various plans proposed by the Conference, or any changes to be suggested, I would ask that they be sent to me sometime before the first of September. Every change or suggestion will be carefully noted and submitted to the Committee of the Board, and through the Committee to the Board itself. This is the time for any of us to bring forward objections, or additional recommendations, in view of the great changes proposed. The Executive Council approved unanimously the entire findings of the Conference. We have sent the details of the Conference to all the leading religious newspapers, and many of them have promised to publish editorials favorable to the plans proposed. We believe that this movement is one fraught with great consequence for good to the entire work in Mexico. But we need the coöperation of all who are interested in Mexico in order to bring about this result."

The spirit of many of the missionaries in the face of the necessity of leaving the well-established work built up by years of service showed a true devotion to the larger cause. Miss Mary F. Turner had helped to develop a successful school in Aguascalientes, which she was now asked to leave, to begin work in a pioneer field. On July 17, 1914, she wrote:

" Personally, I am willing to drop into the work anywhere where it seems best. I am glad to look forward to a work in Mexico with all Churches and Boards coöperating in that work. It is certainly more in harmony with the gospel teaching, and whatever inconvenience it may work for a time for both missionary and Mexican people, the next generation will see a stronger evangelical Church in Mexico."

Dr. William Wallace wrote on August 15, 1914: " I am glad to know, as I had already supposed, that our Board will substantially approve what was agreed on at the Conference. It will involve heavy sacrifices and inconvenience and trouble in rearrangement, but this was to have been discounted from the beginning and in later years will be forgotten in the great gain which shall have come in concentration and more vigorous handling of the work of each Mission."

On September 14, 1914, Rev. N. J. Elliott wrote:

" I have only commendation for the entire report of the Conference and I believe that if the same spirit of coöperation is continued the entire plan will go into operation with the minimum of difficulties. . . . The Mexicans are reasonable enough if you can get them before they get to the revolution stage. I believe we must do all we can to get them to see the reasonablness of the plans, otherwise we will experience a revolution which will go under the name of an Independent Church or Movement which can do a lot of damage."

On November 30, 1914, Mr. Petran urged consulting the native Church:

" As soon as the report of the Cincinnati Conference was published, I sent a copy to all the leaders of our Church in Mexico. All the men in Yucatan, Campeche, Tabasco, favor the plan, in fact are enthusiastic for it. They look for a greater work in the future through it. They feel in a way that they have been neglected and that the opportunities in the Peninsula have not been taken advantage of. . . . The men in northern Mexico

have made hardly any comment. This is true of
Dr. Morales and Dr. Arellano. I hear from them
with a fair degree of frequency, but they have never
made any comment on the plans outlined. I think
that you will find that they will consider the plans
with a large measure of reserve. . . . You will
remember that I have advocated that our next meeting to consider the Cincinnati Plan be in Mexico
City, and one of the reasons that makes me take
this position is that we should not get too far along
before we take the leaders of the Mexican Church
into the deliberations.

" The men most vitally affected in a personal
way by the plans are our men in northern and central Mexico, and so I trust that we do not get very
far in our final resolutions, before we can meet them
in conference and go over the whole matter with
them."

On January 17, 1916, in accordance with suggestions from the members of the Mission, Dr.
Halsey sent a letter to the Stated Clerk of the
Synod of Mexico setting forth the plan and urging
acquiescence and agreement with it, and co-
operation with the Mission in the planning for the
work of the Kingdom in Mexico. The letter
follows:

"NEW YORK,
"January 17, 1916.

" Dear Brother:

" It gives me great pleasure to address you as
representing the Synod of Mexico. No doubt you
and your fellow workers have heard of the Confer-

ence of representatives of all the evangelistic Boards and Societies at work in Mexico, which met in the city of Cincinnati, Ohio, June 30 to July 1, 1914, to consider how best to promote the Kingdom of God in Mexico. This Conference after many hours of prayerful and careful consideration of all the problems involved, adopted a comprehensive plan for unifying all the Christian forces at work in the Mexican Republic.

" The plan in brief aims at reducing competition between the various organizations by a union of forces wherever possible, and by such a distribution of territory that the larger denominations will each occupy certain sections of Mexico, and in this way the entire territory will be thoroughly reached by the various messengers of the gospel of Christ. No doubt it will not be possible to carry out all the details of this great plan; no doubt some of the denominations will find it difficult to adapt themselves to the changes suggested; but we hope and pray that you all will coöperate with us in making this plan as far as possible a great success, and thus advancing the Kingdom of God in Mexico.

" The plan will require time and thought and much prayer before it is finally consummated, but we believe that if each of us enters heartily into the consideration of all the problems, and each shows a willingness to yield all the points possible, and each comes with a Christlike spirit to the consideration of the various difficulties involved, there will result a great forward movement for the evangelization of Mexico.

" I am writing this letter, trusting that you will present it to the first meeting of the synod after its receipt, and that you and your fellow laborers will join heartily with us whose only aim in this whole matter is to advance the best interests of the gospel in Mexico.

" May I add, dear Christian brother, that we feel that the present is a time of great opportunity for Mexico. The people are ready for the gospel. The discipline which has come through long years of suffering and of privation should soften the hearts of the Mexican people and open the way for the teaching of the blessed gospel of our Lord and Saviour, Jesus Christ. May we be glad of the opportunity thus presented to us in the providence of God, and may the blessing of God the Father, the Son, and the Holy Spirit, abide with us all in this critical era in the history of the Republic of Mexico, and in the history of the Christian Church in Mexico."

At a Conference held in Panama in 1916, the Cincinnati Plan of coöperation was discussed and voted upon. Dr. Speer stated:

" There are two very distinct problems involved in transfer of territory: the ecclesiastical problem and the problem of missionary administration. Certain Boards sustain no ecclesiastical relations to churches established by their missions; in such cases the churches may decide for themselves to which Communion they will adhere. It is very desirable that such matters be explained to the members of the churches by those sympathetic to the issues involved. From the standpoint of administration it is for the Boards to determine whether they will give support or withdraw support. The Presbyterian Church faced the same problem in Liberia with the Methodist and Episcopalian Churches and withdrew from certain territory and encouraged the people to affiliate themselves with the other Churches. The people were unwilling to do so and maintained their existence as a Presbyterian church, but without subsidies from the Board. The Presbyterian Board feels strongly with regard to Mexico in just the same way. They would not bring any undue constraint to bear upon churches to alter their denominational affiliations, but they can discontinue the schools they support, the presence of their missionaries, and any subsidies for the maintenance of these churches in territory where they feel it would be wise that there should be a different arrangement."

In regard to holding in abeyance any territorial understanding, Dr. Speer said that in some areas it would work out all right but that in others it would not.

" If certain work is resumed it will be next to impossible a few years later to readjust the territory. The Presbyterian Board would like to cooperate definitely with at least one other Board and go forward."

Dr. Mott spoke on how deeply he was impressed by the way the laymen have regarded the Cincinnati Conference on Mexico, saying that no step has been taken with reference to foreign missions

PYRAMID OF THE SUN AT SAN JUAN TEOTIHUACAN, "THE CITY OF THE GODS"

Built by the Toltecs a thousand years ago (*p. 69*).

in recent years which has so favorably impressed discerning laymen of large outlook and large financial possibilities. They have said, " If this is the policy that is now likely to obtain we are becoming interested." He believed that the discussions and resolutions at Cincinnati had more to do in making possible the Panama Congress than many realize.

He further said: " I honestly believe that the attitude and expressions of the workers right in this room, from Mexico and from the Boards interested in Mexico, will have more to do with pointing the way to the solution of the most obstinate problems, in this and in the other parts of Latin America, that are coming forward in these days, than any other single thing done on these grounds. In other words, we have had resolutions long enough. We have seen the path indicated at Cincinnati, but Cincinnati went one step farther than resolutions. We have said, ' We will take this matter right into the Board rooms and we will apply our principles.' And it would seem, therefore, that if in a concerted, statesmanlike, courageous, and sacrificial manner, we would go forward in ways that we cannot believe we were led into by selfish considerations, even though we might have been mistaken here and there in detail, such action would prove contagious. The difficulties are not without their advantages. These difficulties are going to be our salvation. If it were an easy path we might well distrust it. . . . How do you measure success? By the number and extent of difficulties you have to overcome. . . .

Count it all joy when you find yourself in the midst of manifold difficulties."

After discussion, it was voted:

" First, that we heartily support the Cincinnati resolutions in principle; second, that, leaving the question of the reorganization and realignment of the Mexican churches in abeyance for the time being, we would urge the Mission Boards engaged in work in Mexico in the administration of their work to move as rapidly as possible in harmony with the suggestions of the Cincinnati Conference; and third, that we endorse the proposal to have a national convention held in Mexico at the earliest practicable moment."

Political conditions rendered impossible the holding of regional conferences in Mexico after the Panama Conference. Our missionaries began to return in 1916 and the matter was taken up with the Mexican leaders more in detail.

When the final division of territory was made in 1917 and confirmed in 1919, the churches formerly allied with the Congregational Mission united with the Methodist Episcopal Church, South, and after some delay and after various difficulties had been overcome, the Methodist congregations in the states of Vera Cruz and Oaxaca have united with our presbytery and Mission.

It is probable that in the minds of the conferees and of the other Missions lay the expectation that the churches of the Presbyteries of the North, Zacatecas and Tamaulipas, would unite with the churches of the Missions taking over the field.

This has not happened, however; nor has it been true of the Presbyterian churches in the fields centering about Monterey, Saltillo, San Luis Potosí, Aguascalientes, and Zacatecas. Nor have the Disciples churches united with the Methodists South. The Methodists in San Luis Potosí remain independent under the name of *Peregrinos* or Pilgrims.

As Mr. Petran wrote in his letter to Dr. Halsey, dated November 30, 1914, he expected opposition to the plan from the leaders in the North. The opposition has continued in certain localities. As far as the delegation has been able to estimate and discover the development of the opinion of the pastors and churches, it was somewhat as follows:

In the first years after the Conference they had undergone hard times and loneliness. The country was in revolution. United States troops had occupied Vera Cruz, thus giving a color of belief in our imperialistic ideas and plans against Mexican sovereignty. Then came news that there was to be a change of " ecclesiastical sovereignty." In consequence suspicions were aroused. They resented being transferred " like sheep from one field to another." They felt, though of course unjustly, that this was another incident of American injustice. Several years passed before our missionaries could reach the field again. Up to 1917 the final division of territory in the northern states was not agreed upon and the agreement then reached was not fully confirmed until 1919. The members of the Presbyterian churches further did not wish to change their membership to the Methodist Church or to become baptized according to the ritual of the Disciples Church. These difficulties were avoided in certain of the fields taken over by the Presbyterian Mission through not requiring at first a change of Church membership on the part of Church workers in the service of the Mission.

The Mexican Church is, and has been from the first, a Church besieged. It has had triumphs, but its attitude has been defensive. The very nature of its environment has made it suspicious and apprehensive of any strange movement or plan.

It has had to watch the Roman Church with increasing vigilance. The list of martyrs to the cause of the gospel is long. There have been serious outbreaks during these past years. The Mexican Church has been a people of little strength but of faithfulness to His word and name.

The revolution, though it diminished Roman Catholic persecution, brought in a radical social and labor movement. This has aroused new fears, excited suspicions as to the loyalty of certain men to the Church and even to Christ. Missionaries, pastors, and elders fear this radical spirit among the young men.

The churches in Mexico have been troubled both in prerevolution days and in the present, by an inroad of independent missions, some of which proved real blessings, some menaces, and some a combination of both.

The worker, be he Mexican or American, ordained or lay, has to be on the defensive. Being on the defensive implies that there is an enemy, and the possibility of an enemy's presence casts a cloud of suspicion over every plan, movement, or person that is strange or startling.

It must be confessed also that the spirit of coöperation has not always been present in the relation between our workers and our fellow Communions in Mexico. Proximity to the churches which practice immersion always provokes discussion. The changing of a member from one Church to another because of a change of belief on the matter of baptism or Church government, creates a spirit of competition, at least, if not of active enmity.

We of to-day are paying for the sins of our fathers in this respect. Most missionaries have passed this stage of rivalry in service, but some have not, and among the peoples whom we serve the lesser things assume a false proportion that really disfigures them.

Dr. Harry Farmer, of the Methodist Episcopal Board of Foreign Missions, spoke concerning this situation at the Foreign Mission Conference in January, 1923:

" Some of our Boards have had an interesting experience down in Mexico over the delimitation of territory. For fifty years mission work had been going on in Mexico, but in 1919 we tried to put into effect the Cincinnati Plan, which had been drawn up some years earlier but which had not been made operative. We changed the missionary map of Mexico, assigning one area to the Methodists, one to the Northern Presbyterians, one to the Southern Presbyterians, areas to the Friends, and the Disciples. Soon the Methodist missionaries had to withdraw from one territory with their men and money, giving place to the Presbyterians. In some places this plan worked, and in some places failed. Why was there any trouble? It arose because for fifty years we had been in the business, not of making Christians, but of making Methodists, or Presbyterians, and had been so successful in making denominationalists that we failed in the larger work of making Christians. So when the time was ripe for making a national Church it was not the missionaries who opposed these measures but the Mexican Protestant Christians."

Further the Mexican is jealous of any plans " made in the U. S. A.," and especially of anything that looks to him like coercion.

When finally in 1919 the missionaries of the Presbyterian Church in the United States of America were withdrawn from the North, the ministers of all the Presbyterian Churches in northern Mexico united to form the *Presbiterio Nacional Fronterizo de México*. They resolved to stand fast in the faith and practice of their fathers. This action threatened to cause the churches to break away from the presbyteries of the South, but, thanks to the tact and firmness of some of the older ministers, the danger was averted and the *Presbiterio Fronterizo* is an integral part of the Synod of the Presbyterian Church in Mexico.

Certain very definite benefits have resulted from

the refusal of these churches to be absorbed. They
have become self-supporting and self-governing.
This, as all will recognize, is a very distinct benefit
for it indicates a real advance. From now on the
churches in the North will assume their share of the
responsibility for the evangelization of their districts. Their example will inspire the churches in
the South to undertake similar enterprises. The
plea always is, " We are too poor." There is a
natural timidity both on the part of the Church to
undertake so much and on the part of the ministers
to trust themselves to the uncertain contributions
of their untrained congregations. It denotes the
beginning of the movement for national churches
and even for a national evangelical Church. The
assumption of responsibility in this way indicates
a healthy growth of sentiment and the working
out of the long years of training which the Church
has had.

It is fortunate that this first step toward self-
management was accomplished without, on the one
hand, a break between the Mission and the Church,
and on the other hand, the establishment of a new
denomination. Great praise is due those missionaries and Mexican pastors who were able with tact
and true Christian love to guide this newly developed sentiment and force into sane channels.

The Frontier Presbytery, thus organized, includes the Presbyterian churches of the two former
Presbyteries of Zacatecas and Tamaulipas. It
takes in certain churches in the border towns and
even one in Matamoros and another in Browns-

ville across the border. There are several ministers, members of the Church, who live and work in the churches of Texas and New Mexico.

In the gathering of these scattered forces into a unit, there were several incidents worthy of mention. In Tampico where the Associate Reformed Presbyterian Church has a Mission, the invitation to join this purely Mexican presbytery was accepted by the Church after some hesitation. The local congregation later took advantage of the provision of the Mexican Constitution of 1917 and seized the property by denouncing it to the government. The local government took possession in the name of the nation and handed the property over to the local church for their use. The Mission protested and finally took the matter up with the State Department in Washington. Through diplomatic channels the Mission succeeded in recovering the property.

The article of the Constitution referred to states that Churches cannot hold property in Mexico. This provision, however, is modified in practice by the distinction between private and public property, between that held by a foreign Church and by a Mexican. Full details of the working out of this problem will be given in Chapter XVIII.

The situation in the North has led the delegation to certain conclusions: First, that under all the circumstances it is best for the Presbyterian churches to continue their separate existence as an integral part of the Presbyterian Church of Mexico. That any attempt to apply pressure to them to join other bodies would be unwise and only provoke a spirit of disunion and destroy in part the spirit of independence which now promises so much for real progress.

Second, that in accordance with the practice in other parts of Mexico, where independent churches have maintained their existence, these churches should be allowed the use of the church properties and manses which have been in their possession during recent years. In accordance with this principle, our Mission and Board allowed the independent Presbyterian churches in the North to occupy the church buildings and adjoining manses, although the titles for the property still remain in possession of the Board. This matter is discussed further in Chapter XVIII.

Third, that the Mission can keep its pact as to division of territory by devoting its energies to the work in the South, but still can maintain the exercise of a spirit of helpful sympathy through the synods. We were asked by the Mission whether the Board would consider it within the range of proper service to send teachers north to help in the institutes (for Bible instruction) that might be organized for the benefit of these churches. This question is now before the Mission and should be settled in conference with the other Missions concerned.

Fourth, it was an interesting observation made by one of the older missionaries that the difficulty in bringing about Christian union in Mexico is due to its proximity to the United States, that the

American example of denominationalism in the border states of our republic could not be overcome in Mexico. The American Churches have overflowed into Mexico and brought with them all their peculiar customs and prejudices. There is sufficient truth in this observation to cause thought. On the other hand, Mexican history testifies to an ingrained factionalism.

NOTE: At the National Evangelical Convention, 1924, the Presbyterians went on record unanimously in favor of union with the Associate Reformed and Congregational Churches, and suggested that Methodist and Immersionist bodies respectively unite also in order that evangelical Protestantism might be represented by three great denominations, which could then plan for a nationwide Church if it seemed wise. In addition to this united group there are of course the Baptist and Protestant Episcopal Churches which have not as yet seen their way clear to federal or organic union.

3. The Attitude of the Native Church in the Central District Toward Coöperation

Under the terms of the division of territory, the Federal District, which includes the City of Mexico, became common ground for all Missions. The work of the Methodist Episcopal Church is in a compact field nearly surrounding the district. Our former field in the states of Mexico and Michoacán and Guerrero is now in the hands of the Presby-

erians of the United States. The states of Puebla
and Tlaxcala separate us from our fields in Vera
Cruz and Oaxaca. Hence the group of institutions,
churches, and workers are in part separated from
the rest of the field. This is not a matter of very
great importance, however, as the railroads are excellent and communication is easy. We are not so
troubled as were the friars in the Philippines in
the early days because the Dominicans in going to
their fields had to pass through the territory of the
Franciscans. The delegation found the geographical necessity of passing through the Northern
Methodist field *en route* to Oaxaca a very delight-
ful experience.

As far as division of territory goes in the Federal
District, a division of the field has been accomplished after a long and tedious discussion. The
questions of the apportionment of territory have
therefore been settled in all the republic. Each
Mission is loyally attacking the problems and opportunities in its own field. It is the hope of your
representatives, both in the delegation and in the
Mexico Mission, that the spirit and method of the
Cincinnati Plan may be carried out with success
and a genuine blessing from God.

In the Central District, however, there have been
problems connected with the working out of the
Cincinnati Plan especially in regard to the union
press and paper (*El Mundo Cristiano*). This
form of coöperation has aroused much discussion
and is responsible, whether rightly or wrongly, for
the lack of loyal support of the plan on the part

of the ministers of the Mexican Presbyterian
Church.

In the last few days before we left Mexico City
we had a conference with the Mexican ministers, in
which they were asked to speak in all frankness and
set forth their opinion and criticism of the press and
paper *El Mundo Cristiano,* of the bookstore
and Seminary, and of practically everything that
savored of union effort. They made the statement
that they believed in the necessity and possibility of
a periodical for all the churches in Mexico, and for
a publishing house that would supply the need of
Mexico and South America for religious literature
but they also desired a paper of their own that
would carry the news and the instructions that they
felt unwise to put in a general paper, and in which
they would be free to express their opinion on gen
eral subjects. They were also anxious to help in
purchasing literature for use in our own field.

In conclusion we wish to record our faith in the
genuine devotion of the Mexico Mission and of the
Mexican Church. They have proved, in labor and
in suffering, in prison and in death, in the more
than forty stripes often, in patient endurance, in
courage unflinching, in the genuine perseverance of
the saints, that God has been and is with them
The gospel is a reality to them and the weaknesses
and unfortunate things which at times develop are
in no sense unique; they have been the common
heritage of the Church of Christ from the time
that Paul wrote to the Church in Corinth down to
the present. From the ranks in Mexico have en

CALENDARIO AZTECA O PIEDRA DEL SOL
EN EL MES DE DICIEMBRE DEL AÑO DE 1790
AL PRACTICARSE LA NIVELACIÓN PARA EL NUEVO
EMP.DRADO DE LA PLAZA MAYOR DE ESTA CAPITAL
FUE DESCUBIERTO ESTE MONOLITO Y COLOCADO
DESPUES AL PIE DE LA TORRE OCCIDENTAL DE LA
CATEDRAL POR EL LADO QUE VE AL PONIENTE
DE CUYO LUGAR SE TRASLADÓ A ESTE MUSEO
NACIONAL EN AGOSTO DE 1885

CALENDAR STONE OF THE AZTECS

"Significant proof of their high level of culture and
civilization" (*p. 71*).

ered the glorious army of martyrs, many who
o save their lives would not deny their Lord and
Master. Theirs is a Church that can rightly be
alled " partakers with us in the tribulation and
kingdom and the patience which are in Jesus."

It was the privilege of the writer in the year
921 to visit the work of our Mission in India, and
ne morning as the first promise of the coming day
ppeared in the sky, with some friends we clam-
ered up to the top of the building that forms the
gateway of the park at Agra, where there is situated that wonderful tomb which the world calls
he Taj Mahal. In the eastern skies hung the
wonderful chain of planets that graced the heavens
n November, 1921 — the most beautiful heavenly
display that we had ever seen. In front was the
dim form of the building. While we stood on the
parapets of the gateway, some hundred feet above
he ground, and watched the tomb take shape, its
ines grow clearer and clearer, its color change
rom the gray of the dawn to the brightness of the
full sunshine of the sun-drenched land, beauty
after beauty shone forth, and what had been at
first but a dim promise of a building became in the
full light of day a most glorious vision. We could
not help thinking that in India, and likewise in all
our Mission fields — and we think of it especially
n regard to Mexico — there was peering through
he dimness of ignorance and superstition which
has so long clouded the land, the form of a glorious
edifice not made with men's hands, that spiritual
emple whose symmetry and beauty are manifest-

ing themselves each year more and more to human-
ity; and that the day would soon come when this
finished structure would stand forth in all its
beauty, not the tomb of dead love and of the bodies
of those who had gone, but a living temple, the hab-
itation of God in the spirit, in which should be
united those who have known Jesus Christ.

JAMES B. RODGERS

CHAPTER XVI

THE LAND PROBLEM IN MEXICO AND THE CONSTITUTION OF 1917

LIKE many other Americans, we had heard vaguely of the " social revolution " in Mexico, and more definitely of the provisions in the Constitution of 1917 covering ownership of land and the properties of the subsoil which had been the subject of governmental debate between the United States and Mexico. The aim of this chapter is not an attempt to deal with the question of mining and oil rights of foreigners, but to summarize the agrarian situation in Mexico as well as the economic conditions that have led up to the provisions in the present Constitution which attempt to solve the problem of land ownership. Subsequent chapters deal with political and economic developments since the Constitution was put into effect and with the special bearing of these factors on the work of the Protestant Church in Mexico.

The present Constitution of Mexico was framed at Querétaro, promulgated February 5, 1917, and became effective May 1, 1917, when Carranza was president. The Constitution of 1917 succeeds the Constitution of 1857. The significance of the articles which provide for national ownership of all lands and waters, with the right to create private property as the government sees fit, the provision

for dividing large landed estates and for developing
small landed holdings, the ruling against any re
ligious institutions owning property, and the very
liberal provisions for the rights of labor, can be
better understood if the historical background of
these articles is made clear.

From the beginning of Mexican history the prob
lem of land ownership has been a central and de
cisive factor in the welfare of the inhabitants of
Mexico. Señor Manuel Gamio, Director of An
thropology of the Department of Agriculture
affirms:

" The agrarian question has been the most power
ful factor in the development, past and present, of
the Mexican people. . . . The possession and ex
ploitation of the land has been the fundamenta
cause of the bad economic condition experienced
by the Mexican people from the time of the Con
quest to our days." [1]

In *The Land Systems of Mexico,* G. M. Mc
Bride points out the comparatively small amount
of arable land in Mexico:

" Although the country has a total extent of
767,198 square miles (491,006,720 acres) and in
1910 had a population of 15,115,612, the area under
cultivation is relatively small, being but 30,027,500
acres (about two acres per person), while 120,
444,200 acres are used only for pasture and
40,933,200 acres are in forest. The larger part of
the remainder (299,601,820 acres) is regarded as

[1] Foreword to *The Land Systems of Mexico,* G. M. McBride
pp. ix, x.

virtual waste. . . . Were the greater part of the
Mesa Central and its escarpments (about 120,000
square miles) fit for cultivation, the problem of
the subsistence of this relatively dense population
would not be so serious. But since not more than
twenty-five per cent of its surface is available for
agricultural purposes, it is not surprising that the
use and ownership of the land have here presented
problems of the greatest difficulty. So long as
there were unimproved lands in the restricted fertile spots of the Mesa Central, or so long as the
soil was capable of more intensive development, all
was well. But when the growing population had
occupied the narrowly confined areas and when
once the limit of production with the known
methods of cultivation was approached, there began
an unremitting struggle for possession of the land.
This struggle has been going on in Mexico not
only during the past thirteen years but for generations and even for centuries. From what can be
learned of the pre-Conquest history of the Mesa
Central, it seems that during the century or more
of Aztec domination, and even before, these lands
had been the subject of dispute among the various
Indian agricultural tribes. The keen demand for
land resulted in the development of a well-defined
system of tenure, long before the arrival of the
white race upon the scene. The contest has never
ceased. In these limited districts, Indian and
white, Mexican and foreigner, cleric and layman,
rich and poor, have engaged in a protracted
struggle for possession of the available soil. It is

upon this region, therefore, that attention is largely centered in any consideration of matters related to the land systems of Mexico, either in ancient or modern times." [1]

Many of the present large estates and land holdings in Mexico originated in the Spanish conquerors' practice of appropriating great areas of land and their feudal use of those who lived upon this land. A system of encomiendas and *repartimientos* was introduced, having been employed in the conquest of the Canary Islands and the reconquest of southern Spain from the Moors.

" The encomienda was intended primarily as a means whereby the Spaniards might live in the new land and might utilize the services of the Indians in the development of its resources. At the same time, royal orders strictly enjoined that the persons and property of the natives should be respected by those placed over the various districts. Within a brief period, however, the system lost its original character and became simply a method of land tenure, since the colonists soon came to look upon the districts assigned to them as being virtually their own and to regard the native agriculturists as their serfs. . . . Following precedents, already established in Spain, a system of overlordships came into existence in Mexico wherever the Spaniards found a native people already settled on the land; and, before the close of the first half century of occupation, a large part of the inhabited region of Mexico was held in encomiendas.

[1] *The Land Systems of Mexico,* G. M. McBride, pp. 21, 23, 24.

"The individual allotments were often on a princely scale. Cortes himself was rewarded with a vast concession. It included twenty-two towns (each with its surrounding lands), representing a population of 23,000 vassals. The territory comprising this grant lay in what are now the states of Morelos, Oaxaca, Puebla, Mexico, and Vera Cruz, and included a large part of the inhabited area of the first two. These lands, among the choicest in Mexico, contained part of the rich alluvial lands of Atlixco, now famous for its irrigated wheat farms; the valley of Cuernavaca, to this day the richest center of cane production in the entire country; and the fertile valley lands around the present city of Oaxaca. We can only roughly estimate the extent of the grant thus made, but the king of Spain is said to have remarked, when friends of Cortes asked for further favors, that the conqueror already held estates greater than those of some European dukedoms. The areas claimed must have amounted to not less than 25,000 square miles and contained a total population of some 115,000 people, if we accept the interpretation which Cortes himself insisted upon, namely that the '23,000 vassals' mentioned in the grant referred only to the free heads of families. The royal decree granting these estates specified that Cortes should have the lands and vassals, the woods and the pastures, all waters, both running and standing, the complete civil and criminal jurisdiction — all the rights, in short, which belonged to the crown itself in the aforesaid lands. In addition to these vast estates, Cortes also held a

number of mining properties in Zacatecas, Sulte-
pec, Tasco, and Tehuantepec. His entire possessions were formed into a *mayorazgo* (an entailed
estate) in 1535, so that the property should pass
entire to his heir and remain in the family undi-
vided. As late as the beginning of the nineteenth century this property remained almost in-
tact, and contained 15 villas, 157 pueblos, 89
haciendas, 119 ranchos, 5 estancias, with 150,000
people." [1]

Many other states were not so large but it was
not long after the Spanish Conquest before practically all the arable land was thus divided up and
controlled. Despite the many attempts to free
the country of this system, it is still visible in certain modified forms in the number and extent of
haciendas throughout the country.

" Many of these haciendas are of very great extent; it is estimated that 300 of them contain at least
25,000 acres each; 116 have not less than 62,500
acres; 51 have approximately 75,000 acres; while
11 are believed to have 250,000 acres apiece. The
Mexican hacienda seldom contains less than 2,500
acres — whether situated in the arid plains of the
North, where land is worth little or nothing, or in
the densely settled areas of the Mesa Central
where the price of land is high even in comparison
with that of agricultural lands in other countries.
In places one may see the low stone boundary wall
of a single farm running as far as the eye can reach
over hills, valleys, and plains, and a traveler on

[1] *The Land Systems of Mexico*, G. M. McBride, pp. 45–48.

horseback may journey for several days in crossing one of these vast estates." [1]

" The despoiling of the humble went to such lengths that in 1910, on the eve of the revolution, the greater part of rural Mexico was incorporated in about 8,000 haciendas, i.e., holdings not looked after by the owner in person. In Chihuahua the notorious Terrazas had bought and filched and grabbed and wheedled together an estate of more than six million acres, which railroad trains required eight hours to cross. It was an area equal in extent to the sovereign state of Costa Rica. No wonder close students of history contend that the Mexican countryman was worse fed, clad, and housed in 1910 than he had been a century earlier." [2]

Special problems had also arisen with reference to estates which came into the control of the Roman Catholic Church.

" No accurate statistics are available regarding the amount of property formerly held by the Church in Mexico, but it is generally agreed that it was very large. At the close of the colonial period Humboldt had estimated that the different ecclesiastical institutions controlled property valued at 44,500,000 piasters (some $65,000,000). Shortly after the War for Independence a good authority considered that not less than half of the real estate in the country belonged to the clergy, while estimates made some years later ranged from

1 *The Land Systems of Mexico,* G. M. McBride, p. 25.
2. *The Social Revolution in Mexico,* E. A. Ross, pp. 82, 83.

179,999,999 to 300,000,000 pesos. So extensively were private properties mortgaged in favor of the Church that it is said that there was hardly a big farm in the whole republic which was entirely free from some such encumbrance." [1]

This situation was further aggravated in the last third of the nineteenth century by the concessions won by foreign capitalists involving products and properties of the land, including agriculture, mining, and oil, which, rightly or wrongly, many Mexicans regarded as merely another form of monopolistic control of the country and its resources with no compensatory benefits for individual Mexicans.

The Mexican War for Independence, begun in 1810, accordingly had social and economic, as well as political aspects.

" The chief cause of the social, economic, and racial inequality and the consequent unrest was the system of land tenure." [2]

Although so much of arable land had been appropriated for haciendas and estates, from the earliest colonial history there had been attempts to protect the Indians and guard their communal lands.

" The Laws of the Indies drawn up by the royal council in Spain for the proper governance of His Catholic Majesty's dominions in the New World were very careful to secure to the Indians an opportunity for subsistence. About each village with a church was a square, twelve hundred yards

[1] *The Land Systems of Mexico*, G. M. McBride, p. 68.
[2] *The Land Systems of Mexico*, G. M. McBride, p. 65.

each way, known as the *fondo legal*. Inclosing this was a block, a little less than a league in extent, known as the *ejido,* or " common," on which they might graze their animals and grow their food. About this was a neutral zone, and then came the great haciendas. Each village had its parchment signed by the king of Spain, confirming it in its *ejido,* which was never to be sold, taken, or given away. . . . The encroachments of the powerful on these *ejidos* in colonial times was one reason for the enthusiastic support the Indians gave Father Hidalgo's cry for independence in 1810. But it was chiefly under Diaz that they were lost. The law of 1856 frowned upon communal landholding. The arable common land had to be distributed to the members of the village, and then it was not long before the holders were forced or tricked into alienating them. In a few forceful strokes the Agrarian Law sets forth the result:

" ' The Indian villages having been deprived of the lands, waters and mountains granted them by the Colonial Government, while in the rest of the country the rural property had become concentrated in a few hands, the great mass of the rural population had no other recourse for procuring themselves the means of subsistence than to sell their labor for a pittance to the powerful landholders; the inevitable result being the state of misery, abjection, and *de facto* slavery in which the enormous mass of laborers has lived and still lives.'

" The famous Reform Laws of Juárez, aimed at the vast holdings of the Church, forbade the com-

munity ownership of arable land and thus forced
the break-up of the *ejidos*. Formerly it had not
been lawful to sell the *ejido* or any part of it without the explicit consent of every member of the
community. Now the community was obliged to
divide its agricultural common among its members." [1]

During the past century there have been repeated attempts, both by relegislation and by forceful appropriation, to work out a just solution of
the land problem. The excessive holdings of the
Roman Catholic Church were under attack in the
preceding century. The Jesuits had held a large
number of haciendas "nearly all of them of great
size and many of them among the most productive
in the country." In 1767, Jesuits had been expelled
from the Spanish dominions. In the Constitution
of 1857, when Benito Juárez was president,
Article 27 disqualified civil or religious corporations
from holding real estate. "The clergy of the
Roman Catholic Church and the conservatives,
chiefly composed of the large landholders, in the
three years' war that followed, fought against the
Liberals, with Juárez at their head, supported by
the Indians and the landless in general." In 1859,
Juárez declared the complete nationalization of all
ecclesiastical property. There was much confusion
due to the war and various attempts were later made
to clear the titles involved.

The issues involved are clearly stated by
Ross:

[1] *The Social Revolution in Mexico,* E. A. Ross, pp. 62, 63, 81.

THE INTERIOR OF THE CATHEDRAL OF THE VIRGIN OF GUADALUPE

The sacred *tilma*, or blanket, on which is painted the image
of the virgin is in the central background (*p. 74*).

" As far back as the middle of the last century it
became clear to the Mexican Liberals that popular
government would never have a chance in Mexico
so long as the Catholic hierarchy, controlling two
thirds of the productive wealth of the country,
dominated economic life and monopolized the great
opinion-forming agencies, religion, education, and
charity. The issue was between the thirteenth century and the nineteenth, and there was no evading
it. The ' little Indian ' president, Juárez, in his
famous Laws of Reform sought by suppressing
the convents and nationalizing the vast properties
of the Mexican Church to transform it from a huge
secular power into a religious institution pure and
simple. The Constitution of 1857, which was to
survive till 1917, is acrid with the smoke of this
conflict.

" The hierarchy resisted for ten years and earned
the hate of the Mexican patriots by bringing about
the French intervention by Napoleon III and
the fatuous Hapsburg empire. When, in 1867,
Maximilian fell before the firing squad on the hillside of Querétaro, it was settled that nineteenth
century political ideas were to have their innings in
the land of Montezuma." [1]

The impetus toward division of land into small
holdings received a check in the last years of Diaz's
administration, and when Madero launched the
revolution that overthrew Diaz, " agrarian reform
was the most fundamental part of his program."
Such reform continued in the program of his suc-

[1] *The Social Revolution in Mexico,* E. A. Ross, pp. 136, 137.

cessors in power and in office, Villa, Zapata, Carranza, De la Huerta, and Obregon.

In the hacienda of the present time, despite the strenuous efforts of the past to ameliorate the condition of those who live upon the land as peons there is much still to be won.

" The peons upon a Mexican hacienda are theoretically free. They have been so ever since the War for Independence and, to a large extent, since the early colonial period. As a matter of fact however, many of them are held upon the estate in a bondage no less real because it is sanctioned only by custom and enforced only by economic conditions. In the first place, many of these peons have proprietary claims on the land which they and their ancestors have occupied and cultivated for generations. While, it is true, their tenure has no legal status, it has generally been recognized by the owners of the haciendas and has survived in custom because it has proved advantageous to the landlord no less than to the native. Furthermore, the peons feel an attachment to the land that a stranger unacquainted with their psychology can hardly appreciate. Upon it their ancestors have lived for many generations, have followed the one occupation of tilling these fields, and have looked to the owner as their patron. As a result, the peons not only feel that the land belongs to them but that they belong to it, and a deep-rooted sentiment binds them to the estate. In the second place, the peons have, until recently, been bound to the haciendas by a system of economic bondage which was tacitly concurred in by the officers of the law. This system was designed by the Spaniards, in colonial times, to replace the explicit slavery which the crown prohibited. By a system of advance payments, which the peons were totally unable to refund, the *hacendados* were able to keep them permanently under financial obligations and hence to oblige them to remain upon the estates to which they belonged. Occasionally, indeed, a neighboring *hacendado* might agree to take over the debt that was owing, but, in such a case, the peon merely experienced a change of masters and a removal from the surroundings to which he was attached. The system of payments in advance is prohibited in the new Constitution of 1917, but, until agrarian conditions undergo a complete change, it will probably survive in spite of the law, as it has for sixty years in defiance of the Constitution of 1857. Furthermore, the peons are bound to the haciendas by sheer necessity. Were they to leave, there is no unoccupied land upon which they might settle; and, if this were to be found, they have neither tools, seeds, stock, nor savings with which to equip farms of their own. During the recent revolution, when land was offered free to peons of Nuevo León, few of them were able to take advantage of the opportunity (so residents of the district say) because of this complete lack of capital.

" The daily wages paid to the peons who work on the haciendas have always been very low. . . . Romero, in 1891, gave thirty-six centavos as the average, for the whole country, of the daily wages

paid to field hands. The wages of the peons remained at that level until the close of the Diaz
administration, although, in the meantime, the peso
had sunk to about half its earlier value. At the
beginning of the twentieth century the increasing
demand for labor was making itself felt, with vary-
ing results in different parts of the country, so that
the scale of wages showed a considerable range. In
Aguascalientes, Nuevo León, and San Luis Potosi
a minimum of nineteen or twenty centavos per
day was being paid, while in regions where labor
was scarce, as in Morelos, Sonora, Chiapas, and
Baja California, the daily wage ranged from sixty-
five centavos to 1.50 pesos. The Constitution of
1917 has fixed a minimum wage, but as yet the conditions in the rural districts have prevented the application of this regulation." [1]

" The peon cabins as usual are built on the poor-
est, stoniest land at hand, and the little gardens of
from one to two hundred square yards are by no
means flourishing. The adobe houses contain
from two to four rooms and are roofed with tile.
The floor is usually earth but sometimes flag.
Windows are rare, but the cabins are cheered by
potted flowering plants.

" Compared with some haciendas, San Gabriel is
a paradise for peons. In the State of Michoacán
I saw a chain of low hills looking out over a vast
expanse of corn losing itself in the distance. On
an eminence is an hacienda house, residence of the
administrador, the master no doubt living in Mex-

[1] *The Land Systems of Mexico,* G. M. McBride, pp. 30, 31, 32.

ico City or in Paris. Then, for half a mile the scrub-clad hillside is pustuled with two hundred Lilliputian huts piled up from rocks. A man could hardly stand erect under the ridgepole. One room, dirt floor, no windows, roofed with canes, shakes, or tiles. No bed save a straw mat, no covering save a serape. These habitations of men are smaller, leakier, damper, and more noisome than those the master provides for his mules!" [1]

With these factors in mind — the continuous struggle for possession of land and its produce, the special need of the Indians for protection and aid in this struggle, the oppressive power of the Roman Catholic Church, the four-century-old battle of the peon for his just rights to "life, liberty, and the pursuit of happiness," and the concessions won by foreign capitalists — the underlying purpose as well as the present and future significance of certain articles in the Constitution of 1917 become more clear. Some of the more important and more widely discussed articles follow.

With reference to the general question of land ownership, Article 27, in paragraph one, and in Section VII, reads:

"The ownership of lands and waters comprised within the limits of the national territory is vested originally in the Nation, which has had, and has, the right to transmit title thereof to private persons, thereby constituting private property.

"Private property shall not be expropriated ex-

1 *The Social Revolution in Mexico*, E. A. Ross, pp. 71, 72.

cept for reasons of public utility and by means o
indemnification.

" The Nation shall have at all times the right t
impose on private property such limitations as th
public interest may demand as well as the right t
regulate the enjoyment of natural resources, whic
are susceptible of appropriation, in order to con
serve them and equitably to distribute the publi
wealth. For this purpose necessary measures shal
be taken to divide large landed estates; to develoj
small landed holdings; to establish new centers o
rural population with such lands and waters a
may be indispensable to them; to encourage agri
culture and to prevent the destruction of natura
resources; and to protect property from damag
detrimental to society. Pueblos, hamlets situate
on private property and settlements which lacl
lands or water or do not possess them in sufficien
quantities for their needs, shall have the right t
be provided with them from the adjoining prop
erties, always having due regard for small lande
holdings. Wherefore, all grants of lands made uj
to the present time under the decree of January 6
1915, are confirmed. The acquisition of the privat
property necessary to carry out the above men
tioned purposes shall be considered as of publi
utility.

" In the Nation is vested the legal ownership o
all minerals or substances which in veins, layers
masses, or beds constitute deposits whose nature i
different from the components of the land, such a
minerals from which metals and metalloids used fo

ndustrial purposes are extracted; beds of precious
tones, rock salt, and salt lakes formed directly by
narine waters; products derived from the decom-
position of rocks, when their exploitation requires
underground work; phosphates which may be used
'or fertilizers; solid mineral fuels; petroleum and
ll hydrocarbons — solid, liquid, or gaseous.

. . .

" During the next constitutional term, the Congress and the State Legislatures shall enact laws,
within their respective jurisdictions, for the purpose of carrying out the division of large landed
states, subject to the following conditions:

" a. In each State and Territory there shall be
fixed the maximum area of land which any
one individual or legally organized corporation may own.

" b. The excess of the area thus fixed shall be
subdivided by the owner within the period
set by the laws of the respective locality;
and these subdivisions shall be offered for
sale on such conditions as the respective
governments shall approve, in accordance
with the said laws.

" c. If the owner shall refuse to make the sub-
division, this shall be carried out by the
local government, by means of expropriation proceedings.

" d. The value of the subdivisions shall be paid
in annual amounts sufficient to amortize
the principal and interest within a period

not less than twenty years, during whic
the person acquiring them may not alien
ate them. The rate of interest shall no
exceed five per cent per annum.

" e. The owner shall be bound to receive bond
of a special issue to guarantee the pay
ment of the property expropriated. Wit
this end in view, the Federal Congres
shall issue a law authorizing the States t
issue bonds to meet their agrarian obliga
tions.

" f. The local laws shall govern the extent of th
family patrimony, and determine wha
property shall constitute the same on th
basis of its inalienability; it shall not b
subject to attachment or to any charg
whatever.

" All contracts and concessions made by for
mer governments from and after th
year 1876, which shall have resulted in
the monopoly of lands, waters, and nat
ural resources of the Nation by a singl
individual or corporation, are declare
subject to revision, and the Executive i
authorized to declare those null and voi
which seriously prejudice the publi
interest." [1]

With reference to religious institutions ownin
property, Article 27, Section II, reads:
" The religious institutions known as churche

[1] *The Mexican Year Book for 1922-1924*, pp. 126, 127, 129.

irrespective of creed, shall in no case have legal capacity to acquire, hold, or administer real property or loans made on such real property; all such real property or loans as may be at present held by the said religious institutions, either on their own behalf or through third parties, shall vest in the Nation, and anyone shall have the right to denounce property so held. Presumptive proofs shall be sufficient to declare the denunciation well founded. Places of public worship are the property of the Nation, as represented by the Federal Government, which shall determine which of them may continue to be devoted to their present purposes. Episcopal residences, rectories, seminaries, orphan asylums, or collegiate establishments of religious institutions, convents, or any other buildings built or designed for the administration, propaganda, or teaching of any religious creed shall forthwith pass, as of full right, to the legal ownership of the Nation to be used exclusively for the public services of the Federation, or of the States, within their respective jurisdictions. All places of public worship which shall later be erected shall be the property of the Nation." [1]

Chapter I, Article 3, reads in part:

" Instruction given in public institutions of learning shall be secular. Primary instruction, whether higher or lower, given in private institutions shall likewise be secular. No religious corporation or minister of any creed shall establish or direct schools of primary instruction."

[1] *The Mexican Year Book for 1922–1924,* p. 128.

E. A. Ross summarizes the provisions relating to the Church as follows:

" At first blush the Catholic Church, which has the allegiance of at least ninety-five per cent of Mexican adults, seems to be hounded and perse-cuted by the State. By the Constitution of 1917 it is forbidden:

" To own real estate or mortgages on same.

" To own church buildings or any other buildings.

" To possess invested funds or other productive property.

" To maintain convents or nunneries.

" To conduct primary schools.

" To direct or administer charitable institutions.

" To solicit funds for its support outside of church buildings.

" To hold religious ceremonies outside of church buildings.

" To clothe its ministers with a garb indicative of their calling." [1]

" The Sections referring to subsoil properties, and Article 27, Section I, referring to the rights of foreigners who desire to own property or to secure concessions in Mexico, have been the subject of much discussion within recent months on both sides of the Rio Grande. Article 27, Section I, reads:

" Only Mexicans by birth or naturalization and Mexican associations have the right to acquire ownership in lands, waters, and their appurte-nances, or to obtain concessions to develop mines, waters, or mineral fuels in the Republic of Mexico.

[1] *The Social Revolution in Mexico*, E. A. Ross, pp. 134, 135.

The Nation may grant the same right to foreigners, provided they agree before the Department of Foreign Affairs to be considered Mexicans in respect to such property, and accordingly not to invoke the protection of their governments in respect to the same, under penalty, in case of breach, of forfeiture to the Nation of property so acquired. Within a zone of 100 kilometers from the frontiers, and of fifty kilometers from the seacoast, no foreigner shall under any conditions acquire direct ownership of lands and waters." [1]

Article 123 of the Constitution contains a list of provisions for the welfare and protection of labor, which, to one who knows the history and present circumstances of the peon, is most impressive. These provisions have been thus summarized:

"In 1916 a proclamation was issued by President Carranza making it a criminal offense punishable by death for any workman to engage in a strike. However, the friends of the working class took alarm and in Article 123 of the Constitution of 1917 Mexican labor has been given a charter of rights such as no other labor ever had. Every device that has found favor anywhere is here. The article decrees the eight-hour working day, the seven-hour working night, the six-hour day for working children twelve to sixteen, no night work for women and children, one day of rest in seven, a vacation on pay for childbearing, a living wage, no garnishment of the living wage, enforced profit sharing, cash wages, double pay for overtime,

[1] *The Mexican Year Book, 1922–1924,* pp. 127, 128.

housing for workingmen, accident compensation, safe and sanitary work places, right to organize, right to strike or shut down, enforced settlement of industrial disputes, three months' wages for unwarranted dismissal, worker's lien, immunity of wages from attachment, free employment bureaus, no contracting out of workingmen's rights, social insurance, coöperative building associations." [1]

Some of the results of the attempt to put the provisions of the Constitution of 1917 into effect are described in the following chapter.

[1] *The Social Revolution in Mexico*, E. A. Ross, pp. 114, 115.

DANCERS AT THE FESTIVAL OF THE VIRGIN OF GUADALUPE

"Thus the old Indian impulses to worship by dance and music
had been incorporated as a part of the ritual of the
local Roman Catholic Church" (*p. 75*).

CHAPTER XVII

SOME POLITICAL AND ECONOMIC DEVELOPMENTS UNDER THE CONSTITUTION OF 1917

THE developments since the coming into effect of the Constitution of 1917 have been of national and international importance. There is space here for but the briefest summary of these results, politically, diplomatically, and in the sphere of practical economics. The effects of the constitutional limitations put upon religious bodies are discussed in Chapter XVIII.

Diplomatically and internationally, Article 27 * raised direct questions from foreign nations as to the rights of their citizens, with special regard as to whether or not the provisions of the Constitution should be retroactive. The debate and lack of agreement on this subject delayed recognition of the Obregon government by the United States for more than a year.

On June 7, 1921, Secretary Hughes issued this statement:

" The fundamental question which confronts the Government of the United States in considering its relations with Mexico is the safeguarding of property rights against confiscation. Mexico is free to adopt any policy which she pleases with respect to

* See preceding chapter.

her public lands, but she is not free to destroy without compensation valid titles which have been obtained by American citizens under Mexican laws. A confiscatory policy strikes not only at the interests of particular individuals, but at the foundations of international intercourse.

" This question is vital because of the provisions inserted in the Mexican Constitution promulgated in 1917. If these provisions are to be put into effect retroactively, the properties of American citizens will be confiscated on a great scale. This would constitute an international wrong of the gravest character, and this Government could not submit to its accomplishment. If it be said that this wrong is not intended, and that the Constitution of Mexico of 1917 will not be construed to permit, or enforced so as to effect confiscation, then it is important that this should be made clear by guarantees in proper form. The provision of the Constitution and the Executive Decrees, which have been formulated with confiscatory purposes, make it obviously necessary that the purposes of Mexico should be definitely set forth.

" Accordingly this Government has proposed a treaty of amity and commerce with Mexico, in which Mexico will agree to safeguard the rights of property which attached before the Constitution of 1917 was promulgated. The question, it will be observed, is not one of a particular administration, but of the agreement of the Nation in proper form which has become necessary as an international matter because of the provisions of its domestic legislation. If Mexico does not contemplate a confiscatory policy, the Government of the United States can conceive of no possible objection to the treaty.

" The question of recognition is a subordinate one, but there will be no difficulty as to this, for, if General Obregon is ready to negotiate a proper treaty and it is drawn so as to be negotiated with him, the making of the treaty in proper form will accomplish the recognition of the Government that makes it."

In his message to the Mexican Congress, on September 10, 1922, President Obregon reviewed the attitudes of the two governments as he had explained them to the Congress in his message of 1921:

" Attitude of the American Government: To refuse to recognize the present Government of Mexico, or to renew diplomatic relations with it, so long as it fails to secure those guarantees which, in its opinion, are necessary for the security of rights legally acquired by American citizens in our territory, previous to the adoption of the Constitution of 1917. The Department of State in Washington, proposed to that end, on May 27, 1921, a project for a Commercial Treaty, containing stipulations for the accomplishment of that end.

" Attitude of the Mexican Government: Rather than accept a conditional recognition on the part of any foreign government, for the sake of obvious considerations of dignity and convenience, it would rather ' eliminate ' — through the natural development of its political and administrative program — any occasion for promises which might humiliate it, and continue in this way until the situation be considered sufficiently free from obstacles as to be recognized without loss of national dignity and sovereignty, and to be able then to formulate whatever treaties might be judged necessary for the greater cordiality in the renewed diplomatic relations." [1]

The Mexican Government refused to agree to commit itself in any treaty with regard to its attitude toward these debated subjects, as suggested by Secretary Hughes, and advanced a counter proposal, thus described by President Obregon in his congressional message of September, 1921:

"As the State Department in Washington continued to urge the signing of the Commercial Treaty in order that it might recognize the Government of Mexico, and as it would submit for our consideration a plan for a compact — to be signed after the ratification of the Treaty — creating the Joint Commission for the study and settlement of all claims pending between the two governments, the Executive, ever faithful to that policy of reconciliation which has served as his guide, made a counterproposal calling for two compacts: (1) The first, which would correspond to the general invitation of July 12, 1921, to all governments whose citizens might have claims pending for damage sustained in the course of the Mexican Revolution — an invitation, as I have already ex-

[1] *The Mexican Year Book, 1922-1924*, pp. 73, 74.

plained, based on Article 50 of the Decree of May 10, 1913, and on Article 130, revised, of the Law of December 24, 1917 — which would not have the character of reciprocity, but would aim, as the Mexican Government contrary to the usual conventionalities thus defined it, only to compensate American interests for losses sustained in Mexico; and for greater proof of the good will of the proposing party and of its desire to satisfy all just claims, these claims would be determined (to the greater advantage of the claimants) in a simple spirit of equity. With the acceptance of this compact the Government of Mexico would be implicitly recognized without loss of national prestige; and (2) would then proceed to the second compact by virtue of which the Joint Commission would be established to decide according to the principles of international law all the other difficulties which have arisen between the two governments from the signing of the Convention of July 4, 1868, up to the date of the one under discussion now. With the field thus clear of present and past difficulties, it would be possible to proceed to the study of a treaty, if that be considered an efficient basis for the further development of future diplomatic relations." [1]

Commissioners from the two countries met in conference in Mexico City from May 14 to August 15, 1923, and as a result of these conferences, the two governments agreed to a Special and a General Claims Convention. The Special Convention " pro-

[1] *The Mexican Year Book, 1922–1924,* p. 75.

vides for the settlement and amicable adjustment of claims against Mexico arising from losses or damages suffered by American citizens through revolutionary acts within the period from November 20, 1910, to May 31, 1920, inclusive." The General Convention provides for " the settlement and amicable adjustment of all the claims of American citizens against Mexico, and of all claims of citizens of Mexico against the Government of the United States."

On September 8, 1923, the American Secretary of State issued a statement in regard to the two Claims Conventions. Concerning the Commissions to be set up in accordance with these Conventions, he said:

" The General Claims Commission and the Special Claims Commission which are to be created under the terms of these Conventions are to be composed of three members each, one to be appointed by the President of the United States, one by the President of Mexico, and the third by mutual agreement between the two governments, or in case of failure to agree, by the President of the Permanent Administrative Council of the Permanent Court of Arbitration at The Hague. The Special Claims Commission is to meet at Mexico City and the General Claims Commission at Washington within six months after the exchange of ratifications of the respective conventions, and the Commissions have the power to fix the time and place of their subsequent meetings. The Conventions provide for the appointment by each government of the necessary agents and counsel to present arguments in favor of or against any claim, and the decision of the majority of the members of the Commission is to be the decision of the Commission."

In his letter dated January 15, 1924, addressed to Senator Lodge, Secretary Hughes, referring to the recognition of Mexico and the Claims Conventions signed by the two governments, thus summarized the position of the United States Government:

" In the Department's instructions given to the commissioners when they proceeded to Mexico it was pointed out that the fundamental issue between the United States and Mexico was the safeguarding of American property rights in Mexico, especially as against a confiscatory application of the provisions of the Mexican Constitution of 1917, and that the principal questions arising from this issue related:

" First, to the restoration of proper reparation for the taking of lands owned by the American citizens prior to May 1, 1917.

" Second, to the obtaining of satisfactory assurances against confiscation of the subsoil interests in lands owned by American citizens prior to May 1, 1917.

" Third, to the making of appropriate claims conventions. . . .

" Perhaps I should point out that the agrarian problem in Mexico, the avowed purpose of which is to provide for the needs of rural communities,

involves most important questions from the standpoint of Mexican policy as well as from that of
American interests in Mexico. Provision was
made in the Mexican Constitution of 1917 for the
taking of large landholdings for division into small
tracts, but without provision for the compensation
of the owners. These holdings are often very large,
consisting of from hundreds of thousands of acres
to millions of acres. The carrying out of this
policy resulted in great injury to American landholders in Mexico, and consequently this Government, while expressing full sympathy with the efforts of the Mexican authorities to readjust large
holdings so as to meet the natural demands of the
people of Mexico, at the same time protested and
insisted that if properties were to be taken they
should be paid for. . . .

" It should be understood that an *ejido* constitutes a ' commons ' or an area of communal property deemed to be important for villages and other
communities. The problem presented in the negotiations was with respect to the best manner of
securing substantial protection for American interests against an improper expropriation, while at the
same time satisfying the natural desire for reasonable communal properties or *ejidos*."

The General Claims Convention was signed at
Washington, September 8, 1923, ratification was
advised by the Senate, January 23, 1924, the Con-
vention was signed by the President for the United
States, February 4, 1924, ratified by Mexico,
February 16, 1924, and the Convention was pro-

claimed, March 3, 1924. The Special Claims Convention was signed at Mexico City, September 10, 1923, was approved by the United States Senate and by the President and ratified by Mexico, on the same dates as the General Claims Convention, and was proclaimed on February 23, 1924.

When agreement was reached regarding these Conventions early in September, 1923, formal recognition was accorded to Mexico by the United States on September 3, 1923. Since that date the American Embassy has been reopened in Mexico City and an ambassador has represented the United States there. The revolution, which broke out against President Obregon and against the presidential candidate, General Plutarco Elias Calles, lasted from December, 1923, until April, 1924. The United States Government through the shipment of arms to the Federal Mexican Government contributed largely to its stability and the revolution was suppressed. In the summer of 1924, General Calles was elected President to succeed General Obregon and was inaugurated in Mexico City on November 30, 1924.

In the sphere of practical economics the results of the attempts to enforce the Constitution of 1917 have not been so spectacular or dramatic as in the diplomatic world, although the conception involved is in its own field fully as notable.

" When the work is completed, it will take rank as one of the giant agrarian adjustments of history. In scope the land distributions in ancient Greece, the work of the land commission of Tiberius

Gracchus or that of the Irish Land Commission are hardly to be compared with it. For parallel, one must look to the achievements of the Russian Commission which, in 1861, provided with land the twenty-four million emancipated serfs." [1]

Although it has not been found practicable to carry out in complete detail the economic program outlined in the Constitution, there has been genuine progress.

" Several plans are being followed. In the first place, public lands which had been given out to companies or individuals in violation of the laws are being reclaimed for the nation to be divided up into small holdings. According to official reports, over 15,000,000 hectares had thus been restored to the nation up to the end of 1918.* . . . Something has been done also toward securing land for distribution among agricultural villages on the old system of communal holdings. . . . Many towns have been given *ejidos,* either those which they had lost in past years or new lands. . . . The usual area aimed at for the pueblo is the traditional one square league (about 4387 acres) but many towns receive less and a few at least double that amount. The allotments made to individuals from this group-holding vary from three to twenty-four hectares according to the character of the soil and particularly according to the water supply." [2]

In Michoacán a law was enacted on March 5,

---

* A hectare equals 2.47 acres.
[1] *The Social Revolution in Mexico,* E. A. Ross, p. 86.
[2] *The Land Systems of Mexico,* G. M. McBride, pp. 160, 161.

1920, the principal features of which are as follows:

" All land in the state is divided into four classes: (*a*) irrigated lands; (*b*) unirrigated agricultural lands; (*c*) forests; (*d*) grass, hilly, or swamp lands. No individual or society may hold more than the following: (*a*) of irrigated lands 400–600 hectares; (*b*) of unirrigated agricultural lands 800–1200 hectares; (*c*) of forests 1200–1800 hectares; (*d*) of grass, hilly, or swamp lands, 2400–3600 hectares. All persons who own properties larger than the limit stipulated may select, within a stated time, the portion not exceeding those dimensions which they wish to keep, being obliged to offer the rest for sale or request the state government to do so. The price is to be assessed value plus ten per cent and plus the value of any improvements introduced. Purchasers of the lands so sold may make the payments in twenty yearly installments. Transfer of property and recording it in the state registry shall be entirely free of all taxation. No one may purchase irrigated or unirrigated agricultural lands greater than the eighth part of that allowed the present holders, or forested, hilly, or swamp lands greater than the fourth part of that so allowed." [1]

In San Luis Potosí " the *hacendados* are given a year to divide their estates, and if they neglect to do so the state may go about it. In the western semiarid section of San Luis Potosí the owner may reserve for himself any block of 10,000 acres in his hacienda; in the middle section, 7500 acres; in the

[1] *The Land Systems of Mexico*, G. M. McBride, pp. 167, 168.

well-watered eastern section, 5000 acres. The res
may be taken, divided into single-family farms, and
sold to persons who are equipped to work a farm
The buyer pays down a twentieth of the purchase
price and the rest in nineteen annual installments
The farm cannot be alienated until fully paid for
No hacienda is divided unless there are on file
enough applications for land to justify it. The
hacendado receives the appraised value of his land
plus ten per cent, in six per cent bonds, which constitute a first mortgage on the farms created and
besides, are guaranteed by the state.[1]

" Up to September, 1922, dotations and restitu-
tions of *ejidos* officially reported to the public press
of Mexico had been made in favor of 520 towns
since General Obregon assumed the presidency
Lands totaling 886,156 hectares had been alienated
in favor of 119,649 citizens of the republic, 949 subdivisions having been effected. Only a small proportion of dotations had been made from the public
lands." [2]

As to the general question whether or not these
laws, both with reference to land and to the largely
increased privileges of labor, will work out success
fully, the general opinion of those informed is that
the present generation of peons are not able to
take full advantage of the rights now given to them
but that there is hope in the future.

" On the practical side, rather than the legal, it
is urged by objectors that the Indians do not want

---

[1] *The Social Revolution in Mexico*, E. A. Ross, pp. 90, 91.
[2] *The Mexican Year Book, 1922–1924*, p. 239.

THE BLACK CHRIST OF ROMAN CATHOLICISM

"The verses of Sidney Lanier which speak of the grace and
beauty of the 'Crystal Christ' took on a new
meaning" (*P. 67*).

lands unless incited to covet them by so-called intellectuals; that they do not cultivate them effectively when they obtain them, and that agricultural production has declined because of the agrarian program." [1]

" The social tradition (with reference to labor) from time immemorial has been that of sharp contrast, abysmal cleavage, between the privileged few and the submerged masses. . . . The present Constitution makes a desperate effort to correct the evil, with results that are as yet disturbing to the social organization and the economic outlook. The provisions of the fundamental law on labor are dangerous, not so much because of the ideals sought, as because of lack of discrimination in details or of wisdom in methods employed." [2]

" I have not met one American who estimates that more than a tenth of the peons are equal to farming a piece of land successfully on their own account. The more common opinion is that perhaps two or three per cent might make good as independent cultivators. While all the Americans, whether *hacendados* or not, denounce the inherited land system and agree that the thing to do is to get the land into the hands of those who cultivate it, without exception they put their faith not in the peons but in their children, provided they receive the right kind of education." [3]

[1] *The Mexican Year Book, 1922–1924*, p. 239.
[2] *The Government of Mexico*, H. I. Priestly. *The Mexican Year Book, 1922–1924*, p. 52.
[3] *The Social Revolution in Mexico*, E. A. Ross, p. 78.

In an article in the November, 1924, issue of the Atlantic Monthly, R. G. Cleland discusses the problem of self-government in Mexico. He enumerates the serious obstacles that have blocked the path of self-government, surveying the question of race, in which the Indian blood predominates; the lack of education among the people; the isolation and lack of adequate means of communication from which the country suffers; the failure of Mexican society to develop a middle class; the lack of training and tradition for self-government; the lack of capable and unselfish leaders; and the lack of definite political parties. He quotes H. G. Ward, the earliest British historian of Mexico, who wrote in 1827, "No constitution, even if it came down from heaven with the stamp of perfection upon it, could eradicate at once the vices engendered by three centuries of bondage, or give the independent feelings of freemen to a people to whom until lately the very name of freedom was unknown," and applies these remarks, written a century ago, to the situation to-day.

But Mr. Cleland at the close of his article strikes another note:

" To some degree offsetting these conditions, one gladly confesses that a new spirit is abroad in Mexico to-day which is profoundly affecting the great masses of the common people. It manifests itself in a great variety of ways, chiefly up to this time along social and economic lines. But no one can as yet define this spirit or say precisely what it is. It may be like the wind that comes before the dawn.

It may be like the leaven that " leaveneth the whole
lump." It may be the forerunner of that ordered
liberty and genuine self-government for which the
distressed nation has waited these hundred years."

This new spirit is expressed in the words " pen-
ciled on a pillar of the Bordo Garden at Cuernavaca " during the early stages of the revolution,
when the peons were fighting for the victory of
the " land-to-the-peon " program: *" Es mas hon-
roso morir de pie que vivir de rodillas "* (It is better
to die standing than to live kneeling).[1] As has
been said of a somewhat similar revolutionary
movement in another part of the world, we may
look upon the waste incident to this contest with a
sigh, but never with a sneer.

Toward the solution of these problems, and especially in the contribution it may make toward the
new spirit in Mexico, the Protestant movement
can do much.

The aim of foreign missions is not political, civil,
or economic, but in carrying out the missionary
objective there are political and civil and economic
implications of the greatest significance. The difficulties of any solution of the situation in Mexico
cannot be denied.

" The Indian of Mexico does not leap from a
state of peonage to an independent economic condition as an immediate result of accepting the gospel
or by the process of acquiring a piece of land of his
own. How to find for these people a method of

[1] *The Social Revolution in Mexico,* E. A. Ross, pp. 22, 23, 124,
125.

support that will free them at once from the slavery of the old Church (often they lose their work when they become Protestants) and from the slavery of age-long peonage, constitutes a difficult problem indeed."

The Protestant Church in Chiapas has already had a successful experience in helping its members to achieve the status of landowners. In Chapter XIII, Mr. Coffin outlines the progress that has been made in thus establishing the colony of Eisleben with 130 hectares of good farming land and the attention given to the local situation by the governmental authorities in Mexico City. An official in the Department of Agriculture, in a letter dated November 8, 1921, wrote:

" I was able to see the Subsecretary of Agriculture for the purpose of seeing what had come of the plan for promulgating the colonization law. I was informed they were about to send a law of colonization to the Chamber of Deputies in which it is planned to adopt your system for the agrarian colonies which have been formed under the protection of the educational and religious work of your Mission. (Signed by the Civil Engineer, M. Castellanos Ruiz.) "

Such landowning colonies ought to be multiplied wherever Protestant communities grow up in Mexico.

In education, especially of an industrial type, the Protestant Church ought to be able to contribute much toward the improvement of the standard of living, both material and spiritual, of the great

mass of Mexican people. Special reference is
made to this aspect of educational service in the
aim of the school recently established at Telixtlahuaca by Mr. A. W. Wolfe (described in Chapter
XIX). The coöperative plan for the work of the
Protestant Church in Mexico, outlined at Cincinnati in 1914, advised the establishing of eight agricultural and industrial schools throughout the
country, but there is much still to be done in carrying out this program. Helpful medical service
is being rendered by the hospital at Puebla, but
much more should be done throughout Mexico in
this type of work, which reflects so closely the
spirit of the Master.

Wherever foreign missions have gone they have
included in their range of activities many such types
of service, but it is in the realm of the spirit that
the Protestant Church can make its most liberating
and energizing contribution. Mr. Ross has contrasted the spirit of the peon before and after the
revolution:

" I suspect the main root of the peon's apathy is
social. No future beckons him. Above he sees
glorious beings lolling on the heights in the sun,
free from his limitations and worries, but he finds
no ladder by which to climb to them. Ambition, if
ever it lived in his heart, has been dead in him since
boyhood. He is like a watch without a mainspring
because he is without hope.

" The Mexican masses live without an idea of
what they are missing. With education how they
would thrill to good music! How hang on drama!

But it is their lot to be oxmen; lead grey lives; sit for hosts of empty hours huddled in a serape watching time pass. Melancholy and subdued, uneager, unlit, unstimulated, never gay or bubbling or enthusiastic save as alcohol makes seem to vanish the blank walls of the cell in which they are shut.

" The chief blessing from the revolution is the new spirit. Penury is still the lot of the common laborer, but there is now fire in his heart, hope in his eye. Full well he knows that his children are not to be serfs. The will to be free has broken the fetters which appeared to be forging in the later period of Diaz. Myriads daily go ill fed to work just as toilsome as ever, but they mind it less because, far and faint, they hear a song of good cheer. Sullen or desponding they are not, for the laws and the government are not against them as erstwhile, and they realize that the future is in their own hands." [1]

In immortal verse, whose prophecy has become history in recent years in Europe, Edward Markham has described a figure that might well stand for the Mexican peon to-day, with all the pathos of the oppression which he has endured during these past four centuries, the transcendent transformations now in progress, and the terror that might yet emerge from a misdirection of this whole movement unless the process is redeemed and controlled by the spirit of the One whose service is perfect freedom, who is the Way, the Truth, and the Life,

[1] *The Social Revolution in Mexico*, E. A. Ross, pp. 22, 23, 124, 125.

for peon and patron, for the bond servant and for
the free:

" Bowed by the weight of centuries he leans
Upon his hoe and gazes on the ground,
The emptiness of ages in his face,
And on his back the burden of the world.

. . . .

" O masters, lords and rulers in all lands,
Is this the handiwork you give to God,
This monstrous thing distorted and soul-
    quenched?
How will you ever straighten up this shape;
Touch it again with immortality;
Give back the upward looking and the light;
Rebuild in it the music and the dream;
Make right the immemorial infamies,
Perfidious wrongs, immedicable woes?

" O masters, lords and rulers in all lands,
How will the Future reckon with this Man?
How answer his brute question in that hour
When whirlwinds of rebellion shake the world?
How will it be with kingdoms and with kings —
With those who shaped him to the thing he is —
When this dumb Terror shall reply to God
After the silence of the centuries? "

CHAPTER XVIII

THE CONSTITUTION OF 1917 AND PROPERTY HOLDINGS OF MISSIONS AND CHURCHES

IN the Constitution of 1917, Article 27, Sections II and III, are provisions which forbid religious or charitable institutions to acquire or to hold real property. The provisions are as follows:

" Section II. The religious institutions known as churches, irrespective of creed, shall in no case have legal capacity to acquire, hold, or administer real property or loans made on such real property; all such real property or loans as may be at present held by the said religious institutions, either on their own behalf or through third parties, shall vest in the nation, and anyone shall have the right to denounce property so held. Presumptive proof shall be sufficient to declare the denunciation well founded. Places of public worship are the property of the nation, as represented by the Federal Government, which shall determine which of them may continue to be devoted to their present purposes. Episcopal residences, rectories, seminaries, orphan asylums or collegiate establishments of religious institutions, convents or any other buildings built or designed for the administration, propaganda, or teaching of any religious creed shall

forthwith pass, as of full right, to the legal ownership of the nation, to be used exclusively for the
public services of the federation, or of the states
within their respective jurisdictions. All places of
public worship which shall later be erected shall
be the property of the nation.

" Section III. Public and private charitable institutions for the sick and needy, for scientific research, or for the diffusion of knowledge, mutual
aid societies or organizations formed for any other
lawful purpose shall in no case acquire, hold, or
administer loans made on real property, unless the
mortgage terms do not exceed ten years. In no
case shall institutions of this character be under the
patronage, direction, administration, charge, or
supervision of religious corporations or institutions,
nor of ministers of any religious creed or of their
dependents, even though either the former or the
latter shall not be in active service." [1]

It is clear that neither the Roman Catholic
Church nor the Missions or Churches of the Protestant faith can legally hold or administer property
in Mexico. The situation which the framers of the
Constitution were trying to meet in Mexico and
the historical background of these two sections in
the Constitution are indicated in Chapter XVI.
There is general testimony to the effect that the
provisions are aimed at the Roman Catholic Church
and not at Protestant Churches.

E. A. Ross, in *The Social Revolution in Mexico,*
says:

[1] *The Mexican Year Book, 1922–1924,* p. 128.

" The Protestant missionaries do not complain of being hampered in their work by the constitutional restrictions forbidding a religious body to own church sites or cemeteries or engage in primary instruction. The government has encouraged them to go ahead with their schools and to have no anxiety. Against them the government is not on the defensive as it is against the Church." [1]

H. I. Priestley writes:

" The inabilities to own properties and to carry on religious work, which theoretically limit the activities not only of the Catholics, but of Protestant Missions in Mexico, create another situation in which progress in social work among the middle classes is dependent upon executive clemency. It is true that generous appreciation of the work of the Protestant Missions has characterized the governmental attitude during recent years, and it is likely that this attitude will be permanent, and that the influence of the Mission work will increase in proportion as the service lends itself to education, hygiene, sanitation, agriculture, and elements of culture rather than in religious discipline. There is every reason for generous coöperation of all religious bodies of whatever faith in the work of improving standards of life and living among the masses." [2]

Only twice since 1917 have property holdings of Protestants been put in jeopardy. In Monterey the municipal government took possession of the

[1] *The Social Revolution in Mexico*, E. A. Ross, p. 142.
[2] *The Mexican Year Book, 1922–1924*, p. 52.

Instituto Mérida owned by the Southern Baptist Mission. The Mexicans held this property for about three years. In 1922 they consented to return it to the Mission as a result of a long-continued correspondence between the Mission and the State Department. In Tampico property owned by the Associate Presbyterian Mission was seized and a settlement was reached only after long-continued efforts of the Mission and the State Department.

The constitutional provisions have been directed against the Roman Catholic Church and against foreign oil and mining interests and it may be asserted, without fear of contradiction, that evangelical church and school properties are not in jeopardy.

The present position of the Presbyterian Board and the position we have maintained all along, is as follows: We have not organized a civil stock company to hold the properties of " educational or charitable enterprises "; we are relying, rather, on the deeds to properties which we have long held, which deeds are in our possession. As to new properties, for the present we believe no stir should be made regarding the registry of titles to properties taken over from other Boards or Communions, but that these Boards should deliver to us deeds which they hold for these properties, together with suitable powers of attorney in favor of a member of the Mexico Mission, empowering him to make transfer of the title at such time as may seem suitable and possible so to do. This process is going forward now in connection with the Methodist

Board relating to properties in Oaxaca and Orizaba. With regard to new properties which may be acquired, it will be wise, probably, in the present situation to take title in the name of an individual, just as properties have been held for the Board in the past, the individual executing suitable papers showing ultimate ownership in the Board.

On March 25, 1922, Rev. Charles Petran, the Treasurer of the Mexico Mission, wrote to our New York office giving in more detail the attitude of the Presbyterian Mission toward this problem. The position taken in this letter has the approval of the Board:

" I have your letter of March 9, written by Miss C. Bahr, regarding the transfer of titles of our properties in Toluca, Zitácuaro, Tuzantla and Chilpancingo to the Southern Presbyterian Church.

" We have two property questions in Mexico: one, the general question, and the second, a special situation due to this uncertainty of ownership by religious organizations.

" We have been holding and are now holding our properties in the name of the Board. Our titles have not yet been questioned, and I believe that it is best to continue holding properties in the name of the Board, without, if possible, raising an issue, till such time as it may be possible to get some definite authorization from the government to hold such property as is required by churches for worship and education and the like.

" It may be that sooner or later the government will make a distinction between real estate and

THE MEXICO MISSION AT JALAPA IN 1924

When the Mission took over its present territory, it was stated that sixty missionaries would be needed to man this field; to-day there are but thirty-four missionaries at work there.

properties held as investment for income and profit,
and those properties which the Church may need
for church and school and welfare purposes.

" I rather think that we could make the transfers
in question, as far as we are concerned, but something might happen that would raise an issue and
that would be unfortunate at present. Then, on
the other hand, the Southern Presbyterians have
organized a *Sociedad Anónima* to hold their properties. They have had reputed legal advice in so
doing, but it is more or less of a subterfuge, and I
believe that the decision of the Supreme Court in
the case of *La Piedad S. A.,* a Catholic *sociedad
anónima,* has shown us that the *S. A.* is a false hope
as regards the holding of church property.

"*La Piedad S. A.* was organized in 1902 in
Puebla by the church authorities for the administration of a graveyard, the purchase and administration of country and city property, and the
handling of the capital necessary. It was a means
fixed upon by the Catholic Church for holding and
administering property donated to it. It was intended that the corporation should figure as a commercial enterprise, owned by individuals. The
stock was made out to bearer. It has been proved
by the government that the stock was the property
of the Church and the whole has been confiscated.
It was proved that it was not a real corporation,
nor was it mercantile.

" It is probable that other *sociedades anónimas*
organized by the Catholic Church with the same objects in view will be confiscated. Some one has sug-

gested in the daily press that the government get after the Protestants also.

"The decision of the Supreme Court makes very clear that it is a basic principle of Mexican law that no person or association that has not *personalidad jurídica*, 'legal standing,' as such can acquire legal standing by means of an *interposita persona moral;* that is, by the creation of a corporation ordinarily having legal standing.

"Now while I do not believe in the *sociedad anónima* as a means of holding church property, I believe that it can be used for the organization of the Union Press.

"In the first place the press is a commercial enterprise and properly comes under the commercial code. In the second place a real society or corporation is formed by the transfer to it of previously enjoyed rights, by the parties organizing the Union Press. I would not have the stock made to bearer as now proposed, as it would be more or less an attempt to keep out of sight the owners, which will be the Boards. To my notion, the stock should be made out in the name of the Boards in their corporate capacity. In so doing, there would not be a step in the operation which would not be true to fact — that is, established presses uniting in one in a commercial enterprise. At present, also, no real estate would be involved.

"Under the Mexican Constitution, there is no provision for religious organizations possessing real estate needed for the purposes of worship, education, and welfare work. The Constitution of

917 nationalizes all churches, bishoprics, asylums, eminaries, colleges. All future buildings of this lass will also belong to the government.

" There is a provision for *beneficencia privada,* ut over this form of incorporation the government as very ample jurisdiction — jurisdiction which ould easily thwart the purpose of the founders.

" I am a member of the Board of Administration f the American School, and we have been going ver these matters for several months. At present, he school organization is that of a stock company, *Sociedad en Comandita per Acciones.* The plans or the development of the school call for the acquiring of real estate and large funds for buildngs. The present form of organization is under he commercial code and a stock company exposes he assets of the school to all the eventualities of a tock company, situations in which some one might possibly get control of a large block of stock and orce a liquidation, so that the gifts for a school in perpetuity would be distributed and lost.

" In view of the contingencies of a stock company, and the fact that it is not exactly what is wanted, we are working now on the formation of a new organization not under the commercial code, but under the civil code. It will be based upon Article 27, Section VII, of the Constitution, where t is implied that civil corporations can own property which is exclusively destined to their use; and Article 38, Section II, of the civil code which defines *personas morales* having legal standing as hose corporations which are organized for some

object or motive of public utility or of public and
private utility jointly.

" The basic idea of the new organization to be
called the ' American School Foundation ' is this
Both A and B have a right to open a school obey
ing certain requirements of law and local regula
tions. But they do not want to operate as indi
viduals, so they transfer their rights to C, a civil
corporation organized under the statutes indicated
C with the acquired rights runs the school, conform
ing, of course, to' all government regulations re
garding schools. The American School Founda
tion will have a Board of Trustees consisting of
fifteen persons. We are studying the question
whether or not ministers can serve on the Board.

" The present Board consists of twelve persons
With the exception of myself and two women, all
are capable and successful business men of long
residence in Mexico; some hold high executive
positions. All favor the organization of the school
under the civil code and not under the commercial
The Board, of course, has had the best legal advice
The problem of the school is not the same as the
problem of the churches in all respects, but in some
and I cite this against the *Sociedad Anónima*.

" The Southern Presbyterians and the Northern
Methodists have gone ahead and organized under
the commercial code *sociedades anónimas* and they
have had good legal advice; but to my mind they
are using them as *resguardadoras,* ' safeguards,'
of the property of the church, just what the government charged that *La Piedad S. A.* was doing.

" Some have wondered why we have not gone ahead and organized *sociedades anónimas* to solve our property questions, and so I have indicated some reasons why I do not think that this form of organization will solve our problems.

" I don't see how a religious organization can incorporate under anything until the implication in Article 27, Section VII, of the Constitution should perchance be extended to include religious organizations.

" Till something happens, there seems to be nothing else for us to do but to adhere to the holding of property in the name of the Board."

The alternative relating to school properties, social centers, and so forth would be the organization of a stock company, as one or two Boards have done, having title vested in the new corporation. However, Boards which have already organized such stock companies are not now using them, and the thoroughly informed and capable attorney of the Southern Presbyterian Board, Mr. Harvey A. Basham, of Mexico City, does not advise going forward along this line at the present time. If conditions should change and we found special difficulties in arranging title in any other way, then we could immediately move to organize such a company.

A special problem is involved in the properties belonging to the Mission which now are being used by the Independent Presbyterian Church in northern and central Mexico, known as the *Presbiterio Nacional Fronterizo*. The churches are self-supporting and by agreement with the Mission are allowed to use the church properties although the titles have not been passed, and still remain in the possession of the Mission and Board. This situation and the agreement reached with reference to it was indicated in a letter from Mr. Petran to the Property Committee of the Mexico Mission, dated March 15, 1922:

" In reply to Mr. Phillips' letter of March 4 regarding transfer of titles of the church in Saltillo to the *Presbyterio Nacional Fronterizo,* I would like to make the following suggestions:

" 1. This property has been promised the church for as long a time as it shall make use of it as the place of worship of a self-sustaining church.

" 2. The Mission has no desire to make any other disposition of the property as long as it can be of service to the native church.

" 3. At this time the titles of all church properties are in question. They are most secure in the old titles antedating the Constitution of 1917.

" 4. The National Frontier Presbytery cannot receive property and hold it as such because it is not a *persona moral.* Only an incorporated *persona moral* can hold property, and it is doubtful whether a religious corporation could now be so incorporated for the purpose.

" 5. The presbytery could hold property by denouncement as nationalized church property. It would not belong, however, to the presbytery but to the nation. The presbytery would have the use of it as nationalized property.

"In view of changing political conditions and the continued religious agitation due to the position and activities of the Roman Catholic Church, it would be better to my mind for the presbytery to have the use of the property as property of the Mission than as nationalized church property.

"It can be objected, of course, that the native church cannot trust the Mission. In this regard we are in a weak position, due to the fact that we went against the desires and judgment of a majority of the native church in the territorial distribution in connection with the Cincinnati Plan.

"There promise to be far-reaching consequences of that experience which the native church has had, but as one of those who desire most fervently the development and establishment of the native church, I do not believe that it would contribute to these ends to nationalize the mission property in question.

"6. It must be kept in mind that all nationalized property is subjected to denouncement. In case of development of factions in any church, the faction which had the closest political connection could obtain possession of the property. Possession of any property would be decided by political authorities rather than by the authorities of the presbytery and synod. The property would be subject to denouncement by governmental authorities for any other purpose that such authorities might think took precedence over the church: for school, for barracks, for storehouse. As nationalized property it would be entirely subject to governmental disposition."

Additional Property Needed by the Mission

The two largest and most immediate needs are sanction and authorization for the building of the boy's dormitory in connection with the Coyoacán School. The Halsey Memorial Fund of $25,000 will be made available to the Mission so that it can proceed forthwith with the erection of at least a section of the dormitory building. Plans and specifications have been completed and the Mission has voted for the erection of this dormitory. The balance of $35,000 required for the completion of the dormitory ought to be provided either by a special campaign, to be undertaken as soon as possible, or by considering this item in connection with other important items when the whole matter of using a part of the receipts from legacies for the year 1922–1923 is before us.

The purchase of the girls' school property in Mérida, Yucatan, at $50,000 is the other large and pressing item. Two or three residences are greatly needed as described in the Mission's preferred property list.

For some years the Board has not been able to appropriate any considerable amounts for property for the Mexico field. In view of the fact that we gave up large and useful properties when we withdrew from the North, while corresponding buildings in the South have not yet been built to replace centers and housing accommodations for the transferred work, it is confidently expected that the Executive Council and the Board will make way for

ιn adequate presentation to the Church, during the
ιext year, of needed property and equipment for
the Mexican field. Nothing will so hearten our
workers in this field as the realization that the
Board and the Church at home are determined
upon providing better equipment and new properties for the more adequate care of our new responsibilities, and the hopeful and growing work in
Mexico City and in the South. We suggest that
the autumn of 1925, or at the very latest the spring
of 1926, be regarded as the time when Mexico with
other countries shall be presented to the Church in
the United States in definite states or districts,
in an intensive campaign of three or four months,
with the determined idea in mind of providing not
less than $100,000 for permanent equipment in the
Mexican field.

DWIGHT H. DAY

CHAPTER XIX

SOME ASPECTS OF THE EDUCATIONAL SITUATION IN MEXICO

IT is not possible within the limits of this study to make any adequate or comprehensive survey of the educational situation in Mexico as a whole. Included in this chapter is a statement on public education in Mexico with statistical tables by Señor Moisés Saenz, formerly Director of the National Preparatory School and now First Assistant in the Department of Education. Señor Saenz is a graduate of Coyoacán Preparatory School in Mexico and of Lafayette College in the United States. In the letters written from the field are various references to individual schools in the different Stations. This chapter includes descriptions of three typical Protestant schools and of the educational conditions in their communities. The first is a description of Coyoacán Boys' Preparatory School in the Federal District, by Robert A. Brown, who has been at the head of this school for some years; the second is of the Turner-Hodge School for Boys and Girls in Mérida, Yucatan, by Miss Eunice R. Blackburn, *directora* of the school during the past four years; the third statement is a summary of the aim and principles of the " Work Your Way " School, which has been opened at Telixtlahuaca,

Oaxaca, the account being written by Rev. A. W. Wolfe, who with Mrs. Wolfe was responsible for the establishment of this school in the fall of 1923.

A most interesting experiment in the distribution of literature was carried out by the Mexican Department of Education in 1923–1924, when such classics as the *Iliad,* the *Odyssey,* Plato's *Dialogues,* the tragedies of Æschylus and Euripides, and Dante's *Divina Commedia* were printed, and circulated through the schools and among the reading public of Mexico. Among the volumes thus distributed were the Gospels, the first time that any Latin-American nation has officially recognized the Bible in such a way. This distribution was carried on under the administration of Señor José Vasconcelos. A description of this movement is contained in E. A. Ross's book, *The Social Revolution in Mexico,* in the chapters on "The Church" and "Public Education."

No statement in regard to educational conditions in the capital of Mexico would be complete without some reference to the school, which has been established in the Colonia de la Bolsa, otherwise known as "the thief's paradise." This school is largely self-governing and is a unique instance of educational development in accordance with modern educational principles. In *The Century Magazine* for August, 1923, there was an article describing this school under the title of "The Miracle School," by Frank Tannenbaum.

PUBLIC EDUCATION IN MEXICO

By Moisés Saenz, First Assistant in the Department of
Education in Mexico

Mexico has good schools but not enough of them. This, I think, is the briefest statement of the educational situation in Mexico. The failure of the educational system in Mexico is owing to quantity rather than quality.

One can find examples of modern methods in almost any school one visits and good schools in almost any city in the republic. The elementary schools were modernized as far back as the nineties, and fashioned after the best French and Swiss models. Rebsamen, a well-trained Swiss educator, established good normal schools which served as models for most of the schools of this type in Mexico. The first public secondary school of Mexico, the National Preparatory School, was founded in 1868 by Gabino Barreda, pupil of the great Auguste Comte, and fashioned after the ideas of this philosopher and educator. The professional schools, particularly those of the National University of Mexico, are among the best of their kind, the school of law ranking among the very best in America.

Although her elementary schools are fine, Mexico finds herself in this age of enlightenment and democracy with an illiteracy of nearly seventy-five per cent, and despite her normal schools only about fifty per cent of the elementary-school teachers in

SAN ÁNGEL SCHOOL FOR GIRLS, MEXICO CITY

A TRACK TEAM OF COYOACÁN PREPARATORY SCHOOL FOR BOYS,
MEXICO CITY

Mexico City are normal-school graduates. In spite of her modern engineering schools, her mines and industrial plants are worked and managed by foreigners.

The great proportion of illiterates is accounted for by the lack of schools in rural communities. The cities and large towns are fairly well supplied with schools, and efforts have been made towards enforcing attendance by means of school police. (Education is compulsory by law up through the fourth grade and to the age of fourteen.) The villages and rural districts have been left almost without schools. Porfirio Diaz, dictator of Mexico for a whole generation, was particularly interested in impressing foreign visitors with the educational progress of Mexico, and he established schools in the large centers of population which foreigners naturally visited, leaving the out-of-the-way places to enjoy the blessings of illiteracy.

In 1910, Diaz's last year in office, there were 9752 public elementary schools in the republic (see Table I) with an enrollment of 695,449 children. Counting the children in the private schools, there were 848,062 boys and girls in the elementary schools of Mexico. This was only a little over six per cent of the population of the country. Had every child of school age been actually attending, this number would have been at least three times as great. Even in the Federal District, the center of the political, intellectual, and social life of the country, only about seventeen per cent of the children attended the elementary schools. If all children of school age had been in school, the proportion would have been about twenty per cent.

This condition was far from ideal and speaks badly for the Diaz administration with its thirty-four years of undisturbed peace and material prosperity. But conditions afterwards became worse during the ten years of civil war. Tables I and II tell the story. The proportion of the population in the schools fell from 6.23 per cent to 4.93 for the entire country, and from 17 per cent to 8.23 per cent for Mexico City and vicinity. Many schools were closed, attendance was not enforced, and, on the other hand, the population increased about a million and a half during these ten years.

In 1916–1918 the school system of the Federal District was put on a basis of efficiency never before known. The number of schools was increased over the number existing in 1910 and the attendance was the highest ever reached in the public schools, 104,038 children being enrolled in government schools alone. Unfortunately, owing to the abnormal conditions of the country, this situation did not last and by 1920 the statistics had fallen far below the 1910 standard.

In 1921 the educational budget for education in the republic was a little over ₱10,000,000 (a peso is equivalent to fifty cents in American money), about ₱3,000,000 being spent in the Federal District; in 1922, the Federal Congress alone appropriated ₱50,000,000 for educational purposes. The Federal budget for education in the year 1923 was ₱52,000,000. We have no data at hand in regard to the educational budgets of the twenty-eight states of the republic, but an approximate estimation would put it at some ₱20,000,000. This would bring the total amount devoted to public education in 1923 to some ₱72,000,000. If expenditure is an index of educational improvement we can be sure of progress in Mexico in the past two years. These figures are, at any rate, eloquent proof of the government's determination to save Mexico educationally.

Elementary education is, of course, only a part of the story, although it is the basic part. The policy of the present educational authorities in Mexico is emphatically in favor of the establishment of vocational schools. In Mexico City alone there were, in 1923, twenty-seven vocational schools with an enrollment of 16,510 pupils. In 1922, the enrollment was only 14,207. All over the country the schools are being encouraged to engage in vocational activities of one sort or other.

There are in Mexico, at the present time, four state, one national, and two Catholic universities. The state universities have been established only recently. The National University of Mexico City is the center of higher education and culture in the country. Table III shows the number of schools which constitute the university and the enrollment and teachers in each.

The data just given show beyond doubt that while in the past Mexico did not attack her educational problem to the full extent of her capacity, at the present time she is determined to outdo herself financially in order to provide education for the people.

The National Department of Education has direct control only in the Federal District. Over the twenty-eight states, constitutionally sovereign, the Department can exercise influence only by co-operation and stimulation, although it has the power to establish Federal schools in any part of the country. There are several ways in which the Department has been carrying on educational work throughout the twenty-eight states. It has established social and educational centers for the workingmen; it carries on a program of education for the Indians; it conducts the campaign against illiteracy; it establishes libraries; it organizes summer or winter schools for teachers, and so forth.

There are six outstanding characteristics of educational effort in Mexico at the present time: (a) The fight against adult illiteracy; (b) the vocational schools; (c) the effort to make the children "learn by doing"; (d) the development of the æsthetic life; (e) the emphasis on physical education; and (f) the intensely nationalistic spirit of education.

The Department of Education has a special bureau to deal with the problem of adult illiteracy. In Mexico City and in many centers all over the country, evening classes for adults are given by volunteer teachers. Special methods have been devised and the teaching of the fundamentals of reading and writing is accomplished in a rapid and efficient manner. There are over 7000 volunteer teachers and 336 paid teachers, instructing a total of 13,603 illiterate adults. Even the children in the upper elementary grades and in the secondary schools have offered their services as teachers of reading and writing. Besides the 7000 volunteer teachers mentioned above, there are at present 4,157 children doing this work. This brings the total number of volunteer teachers to 11,418.

Mention has already been made of vocational training. A fine school of industrial chemistry has been established in the university, trade schools of all sorts are being opened, a normal technological institute for training teachers in vocational subjects is under way. The movement has permeated even the elementary schools where the old-fashioned manual training is being vitalized by having the children make useful things. Closely connected with this idea are the efforts attempting to realize in the schools the famous dictum of Dewey of " learning by doing." There are in Mexico City at the present day certain schools where " education through activity " is the watchword.

The Mexican people are by nature artistically inclined. Professor Ross in his recent visit found copious evidence of this, even in the bodily attitudes and postures of the common people.[1] The Department of Education is trying to utilize and develop this æsthetic quality of the Mexican mind. Indian handicraft and designs form the basis for much of the art work in the schools. Folklore, native music and dances are now familiar in our schools. Indian

[1] *The Social Revolution in Mexico*, E. A. Ross, 1923.

blankets and pottery have been made both popular and fashionable through the appreciative propaganda of the schools.

The Department of Education has established also a national bureau of physical education. Old school buildings are being equipped with gymnasiums and swimming pools; new school plants are amply provided with facilities for physical education. Under the leadership of the Department, a million-peso stadium and athletic field, financed by public subscription, is now under construction.

Education in Mexico, just as in other countries, is not exclusively a government function. There are numerous private institutions, elementary, secondary, and normal schools, and even two universities.

Most of the private schools are Church schools, Roman Catholic or Protestant. The majority of private schools are, however, Roman Catholic. Statistics in regard to these institutions are very meager. About all we know is stated in the data given in Tables I and II.

Historically, Roman Catholic schools have been established since 1857, to offset the laic nature of government schools. They were " godly " schools, so their founders claimed, and meant to contrast sharply with the " godless " government institutions. In fact they were, in many instances, centers of propaganda against the liberal tendencies of the government. As the struggle between Church and State became a dead issue, and their separation a settled matter, the bitter opposition of public and Roman Catholic schools decreased until now it has almost disappeared. The government still keeps pretty close watch over them by means of school inspectors but the inspection tends more and more to become a technical supervision for the purpose of safeguarding the public against educational quackery.

Religious teaching during school hours in elementary private schools is unconstitutional; it is likewise unconstitutional to hold religious services or religious ceremonies of any kind in school buildings during school hours. These restrictions apply to Protestant as well as to Catholic schools. These regulations may seem too radical; doubtless they are, but they have to be considered in the light of past history, when the Roman Church was actively fighting the State. The conditions which justified these measures may have disappeared, but there is a feeling among Liberal leaders that were these restrictions to disappear, the Church would again try her policy of propaganda against public institutions. On the other hand it must be said in fairness to the government that there is a wide margin of tolerance in the enforcement of the Constitution in regard to religious teaching and practices in private schools.

At present, private schools are coming to recognize more and more that their duty is one of educational service in the widest sense, rather than of religious propaganda. They are, therefore, cooperating with, rather than opposing, the government. Just as long as they can follow this course of action, they will be serving the interests of the people. The Protestant schools, it may be said, have from the beginning taken this stand. There has been no ill feeling or antagonism between them and government institutions. Of late, these Protestant schools have seen the wisdom of supplementing the educational work of the government by opening schools of different types from those already existing, or in places where there are no public schools.

From time to time, American organizations or individuals, interested in the welfare and progress of Mexico, have asked us in what concrete and practical way the American people may help Mexico educationally. To these inquiries I have answered: By establishing in Mexico a nonsectarian educational institution which would, on a large scale, demonstrate to the Mexican people educational work of the best type, an institution made financially independent, put in the hands of Mexican and American educators, controlled by both Mexicans and Americans, and having for its purpose the training of Mexican leaders. Such an institution should include a training school for specialists in education, a normal institute of industrial and practical arts, a good school of agriculture, and also a demonstration school of elementary and secondary education.

Such an institution would go far towards the solution of our educational problem and would be a source of blessing to the Mexican people.

TABLE I [1]

Showing Number of Children Enrolled in the Public and Private Elementary Schools of the Republic of Mexico for the Years Indicated

Year	Number of Schools			Children in Public Schools			Children in Private Schools			Total Number of Children in Public and Private Schools	Total Population of the Country	Per Cent of Total Population in School
	Public	Private	Total	Boys	Girls	Total	Boys	Girls	Total			
1	2	3	4	5	6	7	8	9	10	11	12	13
1910	9752	2107	11859	395622	299787	695449	80841	71772	152613	848062	13614873	6.23
1920	8161	1061	9222	357067	322830	679897	38037	34432	72460	743896	15069534	4.93
1921	8388	1327	9715	369864	341728	711592	55081	53102	108183	819775	15069534	5.41

[1] Data taken from *El Movimiento Educativo en México*, published by the Department of Education, Mexico City, 1922.

TABLE II[1]

Showing Number of Public and Private Elementary Schools in the Federal District, and the Number of Children Enrolled During the Years Indicated

Year	Number of Schools			Children in School			Population of the Federal District	Per cent of Population in School
	Public	Private	Total	Enrolled in Public Schools	Enrolled in Private Schools	Total		
1	2	3	4	5	6	7	8	9
1910	442	235	677	69919	22110	92029	341516	17.
1920	197	103	300	46191	13018	52209	719100	8.23
1921	306	164	470	85909	22107	108016	875773	12.33
1922	430	162	592	114713	31933	146646	875773	16.74
1923	288	161	449	93646	22970	116616	875773	15.92

[1] Data obtained from the Department of Education, Mexico City.

TABLE III[1]

Showing Number and Kind of Schools in the National University
of Mexico and Enrollment in Each

Name of School	Number of Schools	Pupils Enrolled in 1923
1	2	3
National Preparatory School (preparatory department of the university)	2	2278
Law	1	337
Medicine	1	1702
Medicine (homeopathy)	1	162
Dentistry	1	94
Engineering	1	180
Industrial Chemistry	1	1184
Graduate School	1	880
Totals	9	6817

[1] Data from the Department of Education, Mexico City.

THE EDUCATIONAL SITUATION IN MEXICO, WITH SPECIAL
REFERENCE TO THE OPPORTUNITIES FOR SERVICE OF
COYOACÁN BOYS' PREPARATORY SCHOOL

By Robert A. Brown, Director of Coyoacán

A. *The General Situation.* — The Mexican Government is devoting large sums of money and great energy to the advancement of education in all grades, from kindergarten to university. For the year 1921–1922 fifty million pesos were devoted to education by the Federal Government.

Special stress is placed on rural schools: about 400 were organized last year, and in 1923 the government planned to organize 2000. Missionary teachers are being sent out by the government into the rural districts to go from place to place, establishing and teaching schools. In this sense only are they missionary; there is no thought of religious instruction.

Nearly 30,000 adults learned to read and write in 1921–1923, through this energetic educational drive by the Federal Government. Mexico has dignified education with a cabinet office; Señor José Vasconcelos is Minister of Education.

The Minister of Education will give financial aid to any state which is willing to enter into a " contract " with the Federal Government, which provides that the Minister of Education shall act jointly with state authorities in the direction and inspection of the schools. In this way many of the more backward states have been greatly benefited.

Eighty-two students were sent by the Mexican Government last year to the United States and Europe to complete their professional education. These students receive liberal financial support from their government.

Teachers' salaries, especially primary teachers, have been raised to correspond to those paid in other professions. A persistent effort is also made to elevate the standard of teaching through conferences, institutes, and especially by exacting a thorough normal training of five or six years. Titles are granted to teachers in Mexico with the same authority as those given to doctors and lawyers.

THE HALSEY MEMORIAL BUILDING (UNFINISHED) AT COYOACÁN PREPARATORY
SCHOOL FOR BOYS

Built from funds given in memory of Rev. A. W. Halsey, D.D., formerly secretary
of the Mexico Mission. "Coyoacán is the only Protestant school for
boys in the capital and Federal District" (p. 79).

B. *Missionary Education.* — In spite of the government's zeal for pushing educational projects, there is a large field for the efforts of the evangelical missionary in almost all departments of education.

1. There are not nearly enough schools even in the capital, Mexico City.

2. There are no schools of any kind in thousands of rural communities.

3. In the government schools there is not only an absence of religious influence; there is positive antireligious education. This is especially true of the schools above the primary and grammar grades. A certain man was asked to take the Chair of Moral Education in one of the government schools in Mexico City. Although he said that he knew nothing of the subject, he took the position because of the salary offered. He taught about three classes during the term, remaining away from the classroom for the rest of the time. At the end of the year he wrote a treatise on some aspects of moral philosophy and had it published. Not all Mexican teaching is thus conducted; there are some real teachers.

4. The present tendency of the government is to look with favor upon Protestant educational work. Many of the men who had leading parts in the revolution and now occupy prominent positions in the government, were trained in Protestant schools. The Undersecretary of State, while not attending Coyoacán School, boarded there when a law student, and all his family are good Presby-

terians. The Superintendents of Education in the
states of Tamaulipas and Guanajuato were both
teachers in Coyoacán, and the former is an alumnus.

5. Mission schools must have the recognition of
the government authorities in order to have any
standing with the public. It is necessary to follow
the official program of studies (although other than
the prescribed subjects may be added); to be
under the inspection of the government inspector
and abide in the main by his decisions; and to present pupils of all grades at the end of the courses
for public examination by a board which must be
approved by the government authorities. This matter of recognition by the government is absolutely
necessary as no student will be admitted to higher
government institutions if his certificate does not
bear the seal of the government. Without this
stamp of approval no student, however proficient,
can acquire a legal title to practice his profession.

6. Teachers often carry classes in government
schools and in mission schools at the same time.

7. In all Mexico there is only about one high
school to each state, many of these being unworthy
of the name.

C. *Boys' Preparatory School of Coyoacán.* —
From the foregoing it is evident that there is a real
need for such a school as Coyoacán.

In the Federal District, including always Mexico
City, there are only two government institutions
which may be called high schools. One of these is
commercial while the other, The National Preparatory School, is about equal to our high schools. It

carries its graduates a little farther in some subjects than do our high schools. But it has an enrollment of about 1800 pupils in a community of
nearly 1,000,000 people. Not only this, but among
these 1800 are very many boys (girls are not admitted) who have come from all over Mexico to
attend this institution which is superior to that of
any state. Many of these boys are pensioned by
their state governments. Eighteen hundred only!
Atlantic City, with a permanent population of
about 60,000, has just the same number of pupils
enrolled in its high school!

Furthermore, these are not boarding schools and
so pupils from other places are thrown much on the
streets. The practice in the government preparatory school is much the same as in a university;
pupils study, if they study at all, outside the school
building.

There are private schools, but they are almost
always Catholic and a priest imparts the religious
instruction. Some boarding schools may not be
Catholic, but they are organized purely for business reasons, and the morals of their pupils may be
whatever nature and environment determine; that
is not the business of the school.

Even Catholic parents prefer our schools for the
training the boys receive. Priests influence many
people against the Mission school, but others, more
liberated from Catholic domination, send their sons
at all hazards. Parents and former students always emphasize the value of the character-training
which students receive at Coyoacán. A sheaf of

testimonials might be presented to verify this statement. There is no other Protestant school of high-school grade for boys in the Federal District, nor any other boarding school for Protestant boys in the Federal District or nearer than Puebla or Pachuca. Moreover, there is no other high school for boys, with a boarding department, either government or Protestant, in all Presbyterian territory.

Students come to the capital from all over Mexico. Everything centers in Mexico City. It is customary, therefore, for boys to come to the capital for their education. We are only following the custom by inviting them to come from the " interior " states to attend Coyoacán.

Without Coyoacán our Protestant children would be compelled to attend either the godless government schools or the Catholic schools, and we should probably lose them to the Church.

Coyoacán serves as a preliminary training ground for teachers and ministers.

1. Historical Sketch of the Boys' Preparatory School at Coyoacán. — Coyoacán is forty-four years old. Some of the first missionaries began classes with young men in Mexico City in 1873. A school was organized in 1879 with Primary, Preparatory, and Theological Departments. Afterwards it was moved to Tlalpan, where one of the professors was Dr. Wilson, now President of Maryville College. In 1885, the school was again moved; this time to San Luis Potosí, where it was united with a similar school which had been established in northern Mexico by Dr. Thompson and

others. After two years, it was returned to Tlalpan, where it remained till 1894, closing because
of lack of funds. The expense was considered too
great by some of the Mission because the self-support was so insignificant. In 1897 the school was
reopened in Coyoacán where it remains to this day.

Until 1900 the school owned no land and was conducted in rented buildings. Then W. B. Jacobs,
of Chicago, gave a city block in the heart of Coyoacán. This was a sacrificial gift on Mr. Jacobs'
part, as the money that it cost was just what he
had saved up against the day when he could no
longer earn his living. Ten or twelve years later
than the gift he was killed by a street car in
Chicago.

About 1901, Miss McMurtrie of Huntingdon,
Pennsylvania, gave approximately $5,000 in gold
to build a chapel as a memorial to her mother,
Margaret Whittaker McMurtrie.

A row of dormitory rooms made of the sundried
(adobe) brick were erected as well as a substantial
stone residence for the principal.

In 1904, John H. Converse visited the school,
saw its possibilities and needs, and gave $50,000 in
gold. The Board, with Mr. Converse's consent,
used a little more than $10,000 of this gift for
very urgent needs in the Far East, so that Coyoacán received only $39,279. This money was
used to purchase one and a third city blocks, with
two residences, and to erect the building for class-
rooms known as " Converse Hall."

The Theological Department was united in 1917

with the Union Evangelical Seminary in Mexico City.

It is worth while noting that before Mr. Converse came to Mexico, four or five of the missionaries had agreed to pray specifically that God would lead one or more of the men, whose names were placed on a certain list, to give the school the land and buildings that it seemed to need. The name of Mr. Converse was one of those on this list. Then one morning the Mexico City papers announced to the astounded missionaries that Mr. Converse was in the city. They lost no time in bringing him out to Coyoacán. He said afterwards that he had had no intention of visiting Mexico until he was traveling through the southern states near the border.

2. Coyoacán Boys' Preparatory School To-Day. — There are two courses: (*a*) Last two years of grammar grade — in Spanish called " upper primary "; (*b*) preparatory, consisting of a five-year course. Graduates from the preparatory enter immediately the professional schools. It carries the student a little farther than our high schools. For example, the government preparatory includes psychology, logic, calculus, mechanics, and moral philosophy.

There are 120 students, of whom eighty-five are boarders. About thirty per cent are from Catholic homes. Many of these unite with the Protestant Church before leaving the school. They come not only from Coyoacán, Mexico City, and the Federal District, but from thirteen other states. Lately many have come from well-to-do families, but the majority are poor. Forty graduates of Coyoacán have entered the ministry. Others occupy important positions in business and government circles.

The teaching staff numbers twelve, although not all of the teachers give their whole time to the school. It is a Mexican custom for teachers to specialize and then to carry classes in several schools at the same time. Five of Coyoacán's teachers have classes in government schools where salaries are high. Our principal of the Primary Department receives ₱2,160 per year; the government salary for the same position is ₱3,650. One preparatory teacher, Señor Trevino, receives for part-time work in Coyoacán, ₱3,180; the same amount of work done in the government schools would bring him in ₱7,000.

The charge for board and tuition is ₱40 per month. This is about all "the traffic will bear." It is one hundred per cent more than it was only a few years ago. Many of the students, and often the very best of them, are able to pay no tuition and only a small fraction of their board; while some are barely able to buy their own clothes. The man of whom we are the proudest to-day, because of his Christian character and because of the high position he occupies in government circles, paid practically nothing when a student at Coyoacán.

In 1917 the income was about ₱3,000. In 1922 the income had increased to about ₱24,000. This includes board and tuition. Expenses have correspondingly increased due to cost of food, the teachers' salaries, and to the larger number of teachers.

3. Plans for the Future. — (*a*) To increase the efficiency of the teaching force as there is great difficulty in finding Protestant teachers who are trained.

(*b*) To add a normal course to the present college preparatory. The training of our own teachers is almost as important as the training of ministers. This will require the addition of two new teachers to the present staff. Little income can be expected from those students who will dedicate themselves to this work.

(*c*) To place the present commercial studies on an effective basis will also require another teacher. There is a great demand for commercial training.

(*d*) To lay more stress on the teaching of English, so that the graduates will be able to use it easily in conversation. This will require an American teacher; he might be a short-term teacher.

(*e*) To meet the government requirements for recognition. This will mean adding to our present courses: French, trigonometry, mechanics, drawing, music, biology, and possibly several other subjects. It will mean also the adequate equipment of chemical, biological, and physical laboratories. But government recognition of certificates issued by private schools is a *sine qua non* requirement for entrance into the national university. Patrons are becoming more and more insistent on the school's attaining to this standard: some have withdrawn their boys because they would lose the work done in Coyoacán and be required to repeat it should they seek admittance into the professional schools.

(*f*) To increase the time for physical education, and to acquire more ground so that all students may exercise at the same time. This is absolutely necessary in a school where the boys are not allowed outside the campus except for a few hours a week.

(*g*) To multiply the capacity of the boarding department. Applicants for admission, even when able to pay all expenses, have had to be turned away for lack of room.

To satisfy the foregoing policy the following equipment is needed:

(1) A new dormitory, a real dormitory, to accommodate 100 boys. We cannot hold the better class of boys with our present sleeping quarters; nor is there room enough for those who would like to come.

(2) A new dining room and kitchen to accommodate 150 persons. The present refectory is only a makeshift.

(3) An athletic field of fifteen acres. There must be room enough for the 100 or more boys to recreate at one time: room for games of all kinds, and for physical training under a competent director. The boys cannot be allowed on the streets, and yet they must have physical freedom and physical education.

(4) Six new teachers: two for the normal course; one American for English; one American for natural sciences; one French teacher; one teacher for mathematics and commercial subjects.

(5) A science hall for chemical, physical, and biological laboratories.

(6) A new site of at least twenty-five acres. That is, the whole institution ought to be moved to a much larger site, which would be ample enough for every activity of the school.

The present site is small, cramped, and cut up by intersecting streets into four parts. This makes discipline very difficult, as the boys have to pass across streets from one building to another. Furthermore, we are right in the heart of the town, and it is a cause of trouble to have the Protestant students come into such close contact with the antagonistic neighborhood. The matter of sanitation is a serious problem on the present site. There is no natural drainage.

Coyoacán takes the place of home to her boys. Many parents entrust their sons to the principal with the remark that he is to be father to them and deal with them accordingly. One man from Tabasco, who had no cash but plenty of land, offered to deed over to the school a farm if it would take his children and educate them. The school may have cause to regret its refusal some day, for I believe the land lies over a petroleum field. If a boy takes the whole course that Coyoacán offers, he will abide in this home from about the age of twelve to nineteen — just the time when the character is formed.

No school that is not almost solely mercenary in its aims and practices can be self-supporting. Even those institutions charging very high tuitions are usually liberally endowed. Coyoacán needs an endowment. Its position in regard to local support is peculiar. Being Protestant, it is *non grata* to the community in general. The Bible is used as a textbook in every year; pupils are urged, though not compelled, to attend Sunday school, and preaching services. Thus, its influence is positive and well known. It counts many of its neighbors as friendly disposed but not openly so. Such as are friends dare not give their support to the school publicly. The Roman Catholic Church's opposition is just as strong as the law will allow. The editor of Mexico's greatest daily, who had been giving large subscriptions to the Y.M.C.A., just last year told the secretary that he would have to withdraw his support because of the clergy's dictum. Other large contributors acted similarly.

The constituency of the school is for the most part poor; there is little prospect of great help coming in from that source. And yet the doors must not be closed against this class of boys, as most of the candidates for the ministry have come from just that source. Every year now, from twenty to thirty boys are turned away from the school because they are not able to bring the funds. Every year the school helps about thirty students, in part or entirely, with both board and tuition.

In order that more poor boys may be received, when dormitory space shall have been provided, and at the same time no greater burden be put on the Board, I can see no other way than to secure a modest endowment.

REPORT ON EDUCATIONAL SITUATION IN MÉRIDA,
YUCATAN, MEXICO

By Miss Eunice R. Blackburn, Principle of the Turner-
Hodge School.   March 17, 1923

A. *Local Conditions.*
Data Given by the Department of Education.

Children of school age in Mérida (approxi-
mately) 16,000
Children of school age in state outside of
Mérida 51,000
Children in public schools of Mérida 10,300
Children in other public schools of state .. 39,000
Children in private schools of Mérida 2,000
Children not in school in Mérida 3,700
Children not in schools in rest of state 11,800

What follows is a free translation of paper sent
me by the Secretary of Education:

At present there are no exact statistics on the
number of people in the state who cannot read or
write.   But a safe approximation is that fifty per
cent of the people in Mérida cannot read or write,
while but twenty per cent of the people in the
state outside of Mérida can do so.

Attempts have been made to arouse the people
to an interest in education through special pro-
grams in the schools to which the parents have
been invited.   These have usually been held at the
end of the school year and on days of special historic interest.   Private work has been done by in-

TURNER-HODGE SCHOOL FOR BOYS AND GIRLS, MÉRIDA

"The *patio* was full of roses, and these children seemed like living flowers as they gathered in the sunlight of the courtyard" (*p. 88*).

dividuals especially interested in the education of
the public, also the press has coöperated in this,
as well as a few corporations and the school authorities, but, sad to say, there has been shown
little fruit of this labor. The reason for this lack
of interest seems to lie in the fact that many do
not use Spanish in their daily life and that there
is almost nothing printed in Maya. Maya is not
taught in the schools, because Spanish is the official
language and because there is no reason for learning to read it. The people are indifferent to education because so few years have elapsed since they
were really slaves. The egotism and avarice of the
capitalists have kept good schools from being established and the results obtained from the poor
schools which were established have given no incentive to the Indian to strive for an education.

It is not possible to say even approximately what
proportion of children are without books in our
schools. There should be few, for at present only
one book, and that a reader, is required of the
children. The other work is given out by the
teacher. [This of course means that the child is
not trained to get anything more than he learns at
school, and is in no way prepared to carry on his
studies by himself when his school days are over. —
E. R. B.]

There are at present ten buildings in Mérida in
which public schools are held, which are considered
adequate by the school authorities. The other
buildings are privately owned houses which are
rented for this work. Outside of Mérida there are

about thirty-five school buildings which are public property.

The schoolhouses owned in Mérida were originally planned for but six grades. The classes are so large that sections must be made of the grades, but there are no extra rooms for these sections. Often eighty or more children are in one class.

All of the schools are equipped with blackboards of some sort; pictures showing the history and civilization of Mexico; pictures showing the evils of alcohol; pictures demonstrating " lessons in physics, and nature study "; figures and instruments to teach geometry; and some schools have sets of weights and measures. A very few schools of Mérida, and fewer still of the state outside, have libraries for the children. Even where there are libraries there are very few books in them.

There are no schools with grounds for games, or school gardens.

At present the Socialistic Party is conducting night schools all over the state. An attempt is made to teach those who must work during the day. [In my opinion, the night schools are used chiefly to teach Socialistic doctrines.]

The above is all taken from the report sent me by the secretary of the university. My own interpretation of the situation follows:

A small per cent of the children who do go to school finish the sixth grade, a larger per cent finish the fourth grade. The unsettled condition of the government makes the people suspicious of the schools and the children are constantly hearing adverse criticism of their schools and teachers until they lose confidence. The teachers are supposed to be graduates of the normal school. To graduate requires ten years of school work. Outside of Mérida there are very, very few teachers who have had more than six years of school work. This means that the best teachers here have had two years less than the high-school graduate of our country. The teaching I have seen is so poor that the average eighth-grade graduate in the United States knows more than these normal graduates. They are interested enough in the work in many cases but do not know the mechanics of teaching, and have no good texts. The teachers are poorly and irregularly paid so that there is little incentive to enter the profession.

The field of this school should include Campeche and Quintana Roo as well as Yucatan, because to reach any other good Church school requires a journey of at least two days. Since children cannot travel alone, the expense is prohibitive for the class of people we expect to reach. The very rich can and will send their children to the United States or to Europe for an education. There is also the racial feeling here against the other tribes of Indians in the republic.

In the state of Campeche the schools are inferior to those in Yucatan. In some of the small towns there are no schools because it is claimed there is no money for the teachers although the school taxes have been paid. Except in the city of Campeche they do not attempt more than four grades and if what is reported is true, these schools are really not above the second grade. In Quintana Roo there are no schools worthy to be so called, and very few of any kind at all. It is said that very few people there are able to read at all. The Indians there have never been conquered, pay no taxes, obey no Mexican laws, and really have no contact with Mexico, their imports coming through Belize or British Honduras. Therefore the field of this school is large.

B. *The Turner-Hodge School, Mérida, Yucatan.* — The school was established in Itzimna, a suburb of Mérida, in September, 1918. There were sixty-two children enrolled. The school was established as a result of the work of Miss Blanche E. Bonine. She later married Dr. Breckenridge. There were thirty-two pupils in June, 1921, when school closed for the summer vacation. The school was then moved to the city and at present we have an enrollment of 125, forty-five boys and eighty girls. They come and go, so that to-morrow we may have a few less or a few more. The first year there were three missionary teachers — Miss Bonine, Miss Bergens, and Miss Sage. Since then there have been but two at any one time. Miss May Mc-Lennan and Miss Eunice R. Blackburn are the present missionary teachers. At present there are five full-time Yucatecan teachers and two others giving two hours and one hour a day, respectively. There was a kindergarten until this year but as it did not pay and as we had only a few applicants this year, it has been discontinued. There are at present six grades which correspond fairly well to the first six grades in the average school in the United States, and a seventh grade which is a modified high-school course arranged to meet the mental requirements of seventh-grade children. We are held quite closely to government requirements as to subject matter and courses offered. Government reports have to be sent in once a month and inspectors are sent out at irregular intervals. At the end of the year the government requires an examination from the pupils at which their teachers preside.

The school owns no real estate but is fairly well equipped for the work it is doing.

The general principles and ideals of the school toward which the present missionary teachers are working are: 1. A good school teaching the fundamental branches of education in the first six grades. 2. A good preparatory course such as will prepare the pupils to enter any professional school in the city. 3. A teacher-training department in which we can train our own teachers and teachers for church schools in the small towns. 4. A boarding department in which we can have at least one girl from each small town in which there is an evangelical community, who is preparing to be a leader in the life of her community as a teacher if possible, or as a church worker. These girls are to be taught all the work of home-making, to play hymns, to be at ease, and to know how to conduct recreational activities.

Rev. and Mrs. J. T. Molloy, evangelistic missionaries in Mérida, hope to have an established Bible school which will be really a part of this school, the school giving the ordinary school work to the Bible-school pupils and the missionaries giving Bible classes out of school hours to those of the school who care to enroll.

All of these forms of service we have begun, but we have not been able to develop them as rapidly as we desire, chiefly because of political conditions.

The needs of the school are, first, more American help if possible, and, if not, more money to get Yucatecan help; second, a permanent building for the school. The present building is the best we have been able to obtain in the city. A disadvantage is that it is now full; if the school grows we shall have to buy more property near, or build additions. Nor are the playgrounds large enough for organized games such as baseball, basket ball, or tennis. The advantages are that it is near the center of the town, and therefore near the church, markets, and the homes of children. There are two street-car lines that pass the house. The rooms are well arranged.

Statistics, School Year, 1921–1922

Total enrollment 140   Boys 39 Girls 101
Average enrollment .. 96
Average attendance .

Work given: Kindergarten, 6 years of elementary school work, and a special seventh grade.
Ages of children, 4 to 18 years.

Teachers: Missionaries 2.

> American   1 (full-time), 1 teacher of piano.
>
> Yucatecan   7 (3 full-time, 3 half-time, and 1 one hour per day).

Boarding pupils, 13; *semi-internados,* 4.

When school closed July 14, 1922, there were 88 pupils in school, 60 of whom returned this year.

Year 1922–1923

Total enrollment .... 126 Boys 44 Girls 82
Enrollment November 17 120   43   77
Enrollment September 30 101
Enrollment October 30.. 114
Average daily attendance for September 90
Average daily attendance for October 106

Enrollment by Grades:

| | Total for year | | | November 17, 1922 | | |
	Total	Boys	Girls	Total	Boys	Girls
First	27	12	15	26	12	14
Second	23	12	11	23	12	11
Third	27	10	17	27	10	17
Fourth	19	5	14	17	5	12
Fifth	19	2	17	18	1	17
Sixth	8	2	6	6	2	4
Seventh	3	1	2	3	1	2

Ages of children, 6 to 17 years.
Internados, 8; *semi-internados,* 5.

Children who attend Sunday school, 38. None of the Sunday-school children pay full price, and 17 either pay nothing or owe over 100 pesos.

Teachers: Missionaries
2.

| | American | 1 (Teaches piano and musical appreciation.) |
| | Yucatecan | 5 full-time, 1 part-time |

In a comparison of the two months and a half of work accomplished this year with that done in the same period of time last year, we find that the discipline is easier, the children are more prompt with their home work, there is less cheating in games, in and out of class, and the average daily attendance is better.

The teachers are coöperating better, are more ready to try new methods, and are actually grading the children's written work.

Our boarding-school pupils are more willing and dependable in the performance of their home duties.

In addition to the regular subjects required by law, namely, arithmetic, reading, grammar, geography, history, civics, and nature study, we teach cooking, sewing, manual training, gymnastics, music, drawing, music and art appreciation. Except for the evening Bible chapter and prayer, and the study of the Sunday-school lesson, no definite religious instruction is given.

On Friday evening, from seven to nine, children of the neighborhood who wish to do so come for games. At these gatherings boys and girls play together. On school days, except in gymnastics, boys and girls play separately.

The pupils work for part or all of their board. Thus they are taught to do housework of a practical sort. The larger girls are permitted to make some special dish for Sunday night supper.

We wish to add three more years to our present course of study, thus giving a good general education through the tenth grade. We wish to add next year, or at once if possible, a training school in which we may give practice in teaching to students of the City Normal School, coöperating with the government and giving a special title for the work.

We wish to add these departments for the following reasons:

1. Because we must have better teachers in Yucatan. We have earnest young teachers, but they have been poorly instructed.

2. Because we wish to train Christian boys and girls so that they will be able to conduct schools in the small towns, and thus conduct a Mission school in every town in which there is an evangelical community.

3. Because boys and girls of the Peninsula must have more advanced work. We believe that the key to the situation lies in having the children, under the supervision of competent teachers, complete the first four grades at an early age. They

will be then too young to specialize in fancy work and piano (a polite way of saying " to hunt a *novio* ") and the parents will be willing to let them continue their general education. At present four years is considered sufficient for any girl and for the average boy.

The public schools are not up to our standards for the following reasons:

1. One teacher has from 50 to 150 children in a poorly equipped room. (A blackboard one meter square is considered sufficient for any room.)

2. Teachers lack both knowledge of subject matter and of methods.

3. Because of traditions the teachers have no adequate conception of what the children are able to do or of how they should behave.

4. Teachers are promised a salary of $50 a month but under the present conditions do not always receive it.

We want to do more for the children of evangelical families here in Mérida. We want one girl from each town in which there is an evangelical community. We have now, I think, all who can pay.

If we could have two more normal or college-trained men or women (college training to have included a teachers' course) and $2,500 a year in addition to our present appropriation for salaries of Yucatecan teachers, we think that we could manage this additional work. We have money for the needed equipment.

The "Work Your Way" School at Telixtlahuaca, Oaxaca, Mexico

By A. W. Wolfe, Superintendent of Evangelical
Educational Work in Oaxaca

The projected school in Telixtlahuaca is a proposal to meet needs now unmet in our present educational system. It will be properly neither an agricultural nor an industrial school, but rather a "self-help" school where students may work to help meet the expenses of their education. However, these manual tasks will be so directed as to contribute to their education and, not only to their own education but, as an object lesson, to that of the community.

Our present schools are all in large cities. Few of our Presbyterian colleges at home are so located. The disadvantages of the big city school are as follows:

1. Environment. — The whole moral force of the institution is hardly sufficient to defend itself against its environment. It has to compete with better financed state and municipal institutions. In a smaller place, the school can dominate the town, creating almost a model village that will give students an idea of what their home towns might be.

2. Spirit of Service. — The young people are fed, clothed, and housed in a style not practicable except in the city. As a result pastors and teachers are graduated who will not return to serve in their

home towns and who cannot — or will not — live on salaries that village schools or rural congregations can pay. Self-supporting native churches cannot be formed in this way outside the principal cities.

3. Cost. — The city schools are located where wages, rent, taxes, and food are most expensive; where the student must wear shoes and " store clothes "; where luxury is constantly before his eyes. This greatly increases the cost of education and therefore reduces the number who may be educated. There are at least five promising candidates for the ministry who would like to enter Coyoacán in January. They are penniless. Two such candidates are already there from Oaxaca. Only some six or seven " free " students can be received from all Mexico, because of the cost. In a small town, money goes twice or three times as far. More poor boys can be educated.

We have several fine, young married lay workers who want an education. Only in a small-town school can this be done at reasonable expense.

4. Quantity Production. — The Telixtlahuaca school will not compete with those in the Federal District in point of scholastic rank. There is a vast field, the rural field, that needs teachers, evangelists, and citizens with a shorter training and a smaller earning capacity — but sound religious ideas and genuine consecration — than our present schools aim toward. These people are needed now,

THE PROTESTANT CHURCH AT JALAPA
(*p. 65*).

BIBLE INSTITUTE AND SOCIAL CENTER AT MÉRIDA
(*p. 88*).

they are needed in quantity.   Only a distinct type of school can accomplish the work.

5. Contact. — Schools in the cities are not adapted for contact with village people who are abashed and self-conscious in the city.   One does not get close to them.

CHAPTER XX

THE APPEAL OF THE INDIAN

THERE is no work in Mexico more appealing or more challenging than that which is to be done for the Indians. By " Indians " is meant not merely the Mexicans with Indian blood, but the Indian communities that do not speak Spanish and live in much the same way that their forefathers have lived during the past centuries. There is a sharp line of distinction between the Latino Indians who speak Spanish and who tend more and more to live as the other Spanish-speaking inhabitants of Mexico live, and the Indian who speaks only his own dialect or *idioma* and holds to the methods of life and work of former generations.

It is estimated that although the people of Indian blood in Mexico number nearly 10,000,000, the non-Spanish-speaking Indians total approximately 2,000,000.

An outline survey of these non-Spanish-speaking Indians was made during 1922–1923 by Rev. L. L. Legters, Field Secretary of the Pioneer Mission Agency. In his report, dated June, 1923, Mr. Legters wrote:

" The problem of the evangelization of the Indians of Mexico is in some ways far more difficult than in Central America. In Central America the

Indian communities are more nearly centralized and compact, the distances to be traveled are less, and the traveling is easier, though the mountains are higher; while in Mexico the tribes are more widely distributed and isolated. They are in some instances scattered, part in one state, part in another, and many tribes are running into states allotted to different denominational Boards. For instance there is the large tribe of Othomi, the greater number of whom are in Methodist territory, while others are in the territory of both the Northern and Southern Presbyterian Churches; or the Mexicano of whom there are more than half a million. Large numbers of this tribe are found in states under the care of the three Boards.

" The data given below are taken from Federal reports. These do not give the number who have Indian blood, or who are Indians as we use the word in the United States, designating blood or race. The word is employed in this report as meaning people who do not speak Spanish, but who use their native language, or *idioma*.

" The number of people of Indian blood is near 10,000,000, but the dialect-speaking Indians are fewer, according to government figures about 2,050,000.

" There is one tribe of over 500,000 population.

" There are three tribes between 200,000 and 300,000.

" There is one tribe of more than 150,000, but less than 200,000.

" There are seventeen tribes having over 20,000.

" There are five tribes between 10,000 and 20,000.

" There are six tribes between 5,000 and 10,000.

" There are seven tribes having less than 1,000.

" That these figures given by the government are incorrect, everyone admits. As I have investigated them personally, I have found that in many cases the figures are far under the real number. One man who had helped make the census said: 'We counted only the cities, villages, and ranches. The Indians in the mountains we did not bother with.' There is one tribe of 50,000 or thereabouts, who were entirely omitted. These figures are a minimum.

" A government official, who tried last January to arrange for schools, said of the Tsendal and Tzotzil in Chiapas:

" ' One of the missionaries (public official), who works in the southeastern region of Mexico, Chiapas, has recently reported in a graphic way the semisavage condition of the Indians of that region. Difficulties will surely confront those who attempt to bring these aborigines to accept willingly such teachings as are imparted to them with the view to redeeming them and bringing them into civilization.'

" The Indian Culture Department, commenting on this report, makes the following statement:

" ' If the establishment of schools and educational centers is arduous and laborious in the great cities and important centers of the country where we are helped by persons strongly in favor of education and by the great forces of civilization as well as the facilities of rapid and easy ways of communication, what do you think of the campaign that the Indian Culture Department has undertaken? This is the task of teaching the great masses of aborigines of the whole native territory, beginning with the alphabet and providing opportunity for more advanced education as well as of converting them to the civilized life. All this must be done with rather a small budget and has in the development of its functions many and great difficulties at every step. One of these difficulties is the ignorance of our language on the part of many of the natives, and the belief that every native white man is nothing more than an enemy. . . .

" ' The Indians of this region avoid all contact with the whites. Owing to this, as I passed through their territory I could not do anything but count their dwellings, because at the announcement of my arrival by the barking of the dogs, the mothers and children ran to the mountains with the velocity of deer, hiding themselves in the thickest part of the neighboring woods.

" ' As for the father of the family, he is ordinarily at his labors, and can be approached only by surprise, because he has, in common with his relatives, the tendency to hide himself from any human being whatever until he has identified at a distance the person who interrupts the quiet in which he lives.

" ' They have no industry. They live by planting little quantities of corn and beans. They raise hogs, chickens, and turkeys. . . .

" ' This Indian is rather antagonistic to civilization, and he is very much opposed to all efforts that tend toward his regeneration, therefore it has been impossible to keep government records, since fathers always conceal the names of their sons with such care that the Office of Civil Register is of no use whatever to this country. The people do not register births, and very seldom deaths. They have no cemeteries, but they bury their dead within their own houses, or under the shade of one of the trees which surround the houses.'

"In Oaxaca are found a larger number of Indians than in any other state in the union. From among them have come some of the great leaders and statesmen of Mexico. There are 33,530 Mixi who claim to be the descendants of Montezuma, famous during the days of Cortes. They are still considered the best fighters in Mexico. I was told that there were many more in this tribe than the number given by the government. As we were leaving one place where we had spent Sunday, two men from another town put their hands on my shoulder, saying, ' In how many days will you return and come to our town to tell us more of this?' I replied, ' I shall never return; I am passing this way just once.' What a pity that some evangelist cannot be sent to 33,000 people!

"We passed through the Zapotecan country for days. This is an outstanding tribe in many ways. It is the tribe from which came the great leader and religious emancipator, Juárez. The census is given by the government at 224,863. The tribe is divided into two great branches, the ' mountain and the valley Indians.' One of the rebel generals told me that he had 40,000 Zapotecan Indians in his command during the rebellion. These Indians are the only Indians I have seen in Mexico who are proud of their race. I spent one night in a very fine home in Tehuantepec. They were all very intelligent, clean, and well dressed — the children attending the city school. I heard them talking among themselves. I said, ' Did you all learn Zapotecan? ' They replied in a tone of scorn, ' No, we are Zapotecs.' They had learned Spanish. I saw another man who spoke and read Spanish. I said to him, ' Where did you learn Zapotecan? ' He replied, ' It is my proper language.' I said, ' Which do you like best? ' He answered, ' Naturally I love my native tongue.' I passed through large towns with nothing but Zapotecan Indians, though all were counted as Spanish because they could speak Spanish. How this proud people could be won if some one brought to them the gospel in their own language, and if a man came to speak to them in a language they still love and teach their children! For even though they may be reached in Spanish, there are one quarter of a million who speak no Spanish at all.

" While on this trip I tried to buy a small stone idol from a man who spoke Spanish and could read and write in this language, although he spoke very little of the Indian dialect. I asked, ' What is the price? ' He said, ' There is no price on it.' I ventured, ' Let me have it, will you? ' He replied, ' I cannot, it is my god.' I said, ' But you are

a Catholic.' He replied, ' Yes, I reverence the
saints, but I worship my gods.' . . .

" In the United States there are small tribes of
less than 2,000,000 Indians, where three Boards
are at work. While there is not one missionary to
the more than 2,000,000 in Mexico, in the United
States there are 444 ordained Protestant ministers,
202 Catholic priests, and more than 800 Protestant
helpers to 340,000 people with Indian blood. . . .

" As one Indian was being told of the love
of God and death of Jesus for men, he said,
' That must have happened at least six months
ago,' and when he was told, ' No, two thousand
years ago,' he fell backward as though struck in
the face. ' Two thousand years ago, and we never
heard it! ' "

Rev. Paul Burgess, of the Guatemala Mission
of our Church, has performed conspicuous service
in behalf of the non-Spanish-speaking Indians in
Guatemala. On October 16, 1922, he wrote to
New York stating clearly some of the aspects of
this work:

" It is good to know that the Board has the vision
of the need of the Indian and is pushing forward
plans for his evangelization. Just at present this
work is in the pioneer stage and so far I have
not seen that it will be possible to take any short
cuts. Missionary work among these Indian tribes
will, I suppose, follow the lines it has followed elsewhere, beginning with the missionary apostle who
learns the Indian language and gives the Word
to the people in their own tongue. Just now it

seems to me our chief aim in this most important work should be to secure such missionaries for the different tribes.

" Of course we should not overlook the fact that the close relation of the various Indian tribes to the Spanish civilization greatly modifies our problems. On the one hand it facilitates our work among the Indians to a certain extent, as there is always a fairly large group of Indians in every tribe who understand Spanish and can be reached through the Spanish-speaking missionary and the Spanish Bible. These in turn may evangelize their fellows in their native language and so the work may be carried on even without the missionary's learning the Indian language. But our experience has been that these Indian evangelists are unable adequately to grapple with many problems which present themselves. These are often linguistic. They do not understand Spanish well. Just yesterday I found that one of our oldest and most trusted Indian evangelists had been rendering Mark 2: 11, ' Arise, take your milk, and go to your house,' due to the likeness of *lecho,* ' bed,' and *leche,* ' milk,' in Spanish. They also are unable to find adequate words in their own language or to form them so as to express many Biblical ideas. So they use the Spanish words. The Indian evangelist almost inevitably, instead of growing closer to his people, begins to emulate the Spanish evangelist, to desire to preach to Spanish congregations, and to adopt Spanish customs and dress, all of which may be all very well but it tends to identify the gospel in the eyes of the Indians, who remain faithful to the tribe and its language and customs, with the Spanish exploiter. The gospel has thus come to be just one more element of disintegration preying on Indian civilization. Personally, I do not think that the Indian civilization has any ultimate future. It will in all probability be absorbed by the Spanish. But there are millions of Indians who can never be evangelized in Spanish to-day. Every reason that can be advanced for missions to the Italians, Bohemians, and Poles of the United States in their own languages, can be adduced in favor of distinctive mission work to the Indians of Latin America to-day."

Elsewhere in this volume, in the chapters that describe the work in Chiapas and in Oaxaca, there are various references to the growth and promise of the work among the Indians in these two states. In Oaxaca, Rev. and Mrs. L. P. Van Slyke have decided to give themselves completely to the service of the Indians of the Zapotecs and the Serranos. Their decision was reached only after long consideration and after actual experimentation in taking Zapotecan boys into the hostel which they maintained in their own home in Oaxaca City. On August 16, 1923, Mr. Van Slyke wrote to the Executive Committee of the Mexico Mission giving reasons for their desire to enter the Indian service and grounds for their decision to begin work at Yatzachi, a three days' trip by mule in the mountains north of Oaxaca City. Mr. Van Slyke's statement follows:

" Statement of reasons for transfer of Mr. and Mrs. L. P. Van Slyke to the village of Yatzachi el Bajo in the Sierra of Oaxaca for work among the Zapotecan Indians in the Indian language:

" No other state in Mexico, except Chiapas, has a problem of Indian evangelization even approaching the magnitude of that which we find in Oaxaca. Chiapas has about 400,000 Indians, most of whom speak very little Spanish, but Oaxaca has over 500,000. These are the figures given by the census of 1910, and are relatively accurate for the present time. Many of these Indians speak a certain amount of Spanish, but are much more at home in their native language. In some sections the Indian language is falling into disuse, but in a great many parts of the country it will be another century before any great change is seen.

" There are two main divisions of the Indian race in Oaxaca, the Zapotecs and the Mixtecs. Of Zapotecs there are probably between 250,000 and 300,000; and of Mixtecs, about 150,000. Two or three smaller tribes number 20,000 or 30,000 each, and some very small groups of a few thousand each complete the list. The Indians of the same race do not all speak exactly the same language; indeed, the language varies greatly from district to district, and even from one village to another. However, the backbone of the language remains the same. The Zapotecan race has three main divisions, the Zapotecs of the valley, the Serranos, and the Zapotecs of Tehuantepec. Men from different divisions do not understand each other readily at first, though they find it possible to pick up each other's dialect. But all the Serranos seem able to understand each other fairly well, in spite of differences of pronunciation.

" The Zapotecan race seems to be naturally strong, industrious, intelligent, and of real promise. Benito Juárez was a full-blooded Zapotec of the Sierra of Ixtlan. The great ruins at Mitla are the relics of a notable Zapotecan civilization of pre-Spanish times. The Zapotecs are known for their desire for the education of their children, and they seem less priest-ridden than most of the other Indians.

" An important element in the missionary situation in this state is its geography. It is practically all mountains. The extent of territory made available by the railroad is relatively insignificant. The missionary is compelled to use much time and energy simply in getting to the different parts of his field. The result is a lack of proper supervision, and great delay in the work. Ideally, concentrating most of the missionaries of the state in the capital city would be our policy, but this policy is not suited to the state of Oaxaca, because of the lack of railroads, ordinary automobile roads, and the consequent inaccessibility of different sections of the state. It takes two days of the hardest kind of horseback travel to reach our congregation in the Sierra. The missionary thus loses four days of precious time whenever he makes the trip. With a shortage of reliable native workers, I have been compelled to do the work of a native preacher in this remote district. The same thing is true of the state of Chiapas. Those who have traveled through the length and breadth of the state on horseback, and therefore know whereof they speak, assert that there is no one center from which the work could be efficiently carried on. The city of Oaxaca should be made as important and strong a center of work as possible, but it cannot with efficiency be made the residence of all the evangelistic missionaries of the state.

" Up to the present time all evangelistic work in our Mission has been carried on in the Spanish language or, in certain places, by means of Indian interpreters. No missionary has learned an Indian language, and no concerted effort has been made to bring the more important parts of the Bible to the Indians in their own language. I know that some translations exist, but the Spanish work has so overshadowed the work among the Indians that no persistent effort has been made, to my knowledge, to follow out a plan of evangelism in the native languages. And since our plan proposes a new departure, and is in the nature of an experiment, it is important to see clearly what reasons there are for thinking such a radical departure necessary.

" There are two principal reasons why the gospel should be brought to these Indians in their own language. The first is that they will understand and accept it much more quickly than if it comes through an interpreter. I will deal later with the question of why we cannot leave the work mainly

to selected Indians whom we might train. With
the few words of Zapotecan that I possess, I can
win people's confidence much more quickly.   I
have seen children's faces change from distrust and
fear to smiles of friendliness at two words spoken
in their language. It is a great surprise to these
people to hear a white man speak to them in their
language, and it pleases them immensely. We can
win people's friendship and confidence and love if
we can talk their language, as we never could without it, and this is the strongest ground from which
to appeal to them for Christ. Through personal
friendship for us, they can be led to personal faith
in the Master.

"The best of interpreters cannot transmit unin-
jured the message one would give. His voice almost never expresses the shades of feeling which the
missionary himself puts into his words. One never
knows whether the interpreter is interpreting truly,
or making up explanations of his own. At times
the truth can become seriously twisted in passing
through the mind and lips of an interpreter, even
if he be a trained Christian. It is much harder
to translate Spanish into Zapotecan than it is to
translate English into Spanish. The preacher
should be able to think in Zapotecan, and not expect a slow-witted Indian, who does not know
Spanish even as well as the missionary himself, to
perform the mental gymnastics and somersaults
necessary to transfer the message into the Indian
language.

"The second reason is even more fundamental.

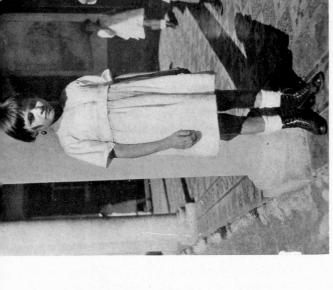

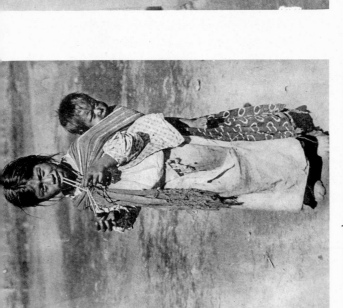

TWO OF MEXICO'S MANY CHILDREN WHO NEED
LOVE AND CARE

ANGELITA — "LITTLE ANGEL"
In the Turner-Hodge School in Mérida.

A CONTRAST IN MEXICAN CHILD LIFE

"Some of these children had come from low and squalid surroundings; they seemed full of
happiness and the light-heartedness of well-protected freedom" (*p. 88*)

It is this: a direct, personal knowledge of vital sections of the Bible has been found to be the only solid foundation for Christian character, and the temporary, makeshift translations made by an Indian are not equal to the task. One who knows well the work among the Indians in the United States has told me personally that in the only three Missions where a really strong, vigorous native church has been founded, the Bible, or large sections of it, has been given the people in their own language. I think we can take it as a well-established principle in missionary work that the Bible, or its more directly practical and spiritual parts translated into the language of the people, is essential to the founding of strong Christian character in the individual convert or in the new native church.

"We all accept this general principle without discussion, but a difference of opinion enters when it is held that it is necessary to give the Bible to the Indians in their own language, rather than to follow the present policy of doing the best we can for the older generation through interpreters, teaching the young people Spanish, and giving them the Spanish Bible which surely presents the gospel far more adequately than any translation into the Indian language could. To some it would seem as though this plan for teaching the Bible in Indian dialect were a step in the wrong direction; that what we should emphasize should be the education of all in Spanish, and that nothing should be done to increase or perpetuate the use of the Indian languages. Or if it should be agreed that such translation is advisable, why not leave it to a well-trained native Christian, who must take a large share in the work of translation even if the missionary has learned the language and is making the translation himself? These are perfectly fair objections, but not unanswerable.

"In the first place, even under the most favorable conditions and supposing in operation the most extensive program of education that our Mission and the government combined could finance and man, it would take anywhere from fifty to a hundred years in order to give the majority of the new generation a working knowledge of simple Spanish. In the meantime, what is going to happen to the present generation and a large part of even the coming generation? Unless the Bible can be read to them in their own language and the gospel preached to them in their own language, the vast majority of these people will die without Christ. Given the Gospels translated into the Indian language and young men trained to read them to the people and to preach in their language, under the supervision of a missionary who knows the language, who knows the districts thoroughly from personal visitation, and who knows intimately the life of the people, these great groups of Indians can be evangelized in this generation, and a strong native Church can be established. But if we continue to try to reach the Indians with a ten-foot pole, as we have done up to the present time, real evangelization will be indefinitely postponed. I, for one, do not like to think of being responsible, because of unwillingness to go to the trouble of living among the people, learning their language, and doing the work of translation, for the failure to reach thousands upon thousands of Indians now living.

"In the second place, in the remote district of Villa Alta, where we think of living, it will take an indefinite length of time to supplant the use of the Indian language in the home and among the people in general. Two powerful causes unite to perpetuate the use of the native tongue: the girls' lack of education, and the lack of communication. As long as the majority of girls receive no education and fail to learn Spanish, the *idioma*, as all the Indian dialects are called, will continue to be the language of the home, and consequently the prevailing speech. Instead of conquering the problem once and for all, we will have it to do all over again with each new generation of children, unless the mother learns and speaks Spanish in the home. And until good roads, I mean auto roads, are opened, and there is more going to and fro, and a greater influx of strangers speaking Spanish, the process of Spanishizing will be greatly retarded. No one can prophesy when such roads will be built. At present some villages are much less isolated and have more Spanish culture than others.

"The exact bearing of this upon the translation of parts of the Bible into the *idioma* is the following: As long as the *idioma* is the language of the home, of infancy and boyhood or girlhood, even

teaching Spanish to the young people will not make
the Bible appeal to them as strongly in Spanish as
it would in their own language. This is simply a
matter of ordinary psychology. We know that our
English Bible has a tenderness, a gripping appeal,
a comforting tone for us in the words which we
learned in our homes that it cannot have in any
other language, however well we may master it.
However we may interpret the ' gift of tongues '
at Pentecost, there is presented there a very true
aspect of the work of evangelization: each man
heard the gospel in his own native tongue. I have
been told that educated young Indians in the
United States, who can read English just as well
as you or I, prefer to read the Bible in the tongue
they learned as babies. Until Spanish becomes the
language learned in childhood in the home, it cannot
reach the people's hearts so well as their own
language.

" Another psychological element in the case is
this: Spanish is the language of the dominant race,
of conquerors, exploiters, and rulers. This influence is undoubtedly entirely unconscious and in
many cases does not exist, but I think it is important enough not to be overlooked.

" I do not wish it thought that our desire to learn
the language and carry on the work directly in the
idioma is based solely on the idea of translating
important parts of the Bible. We believe that in-
timate contact with the people, entering into their
life, and to a certain extent, sharing their conditions of living will go far toward winning them to

Christ. If no formal translation were to be done, we would nevertheless wish to dedicate our whole time to the Indian work, learn the language, and live among them. Nothing can impress them with our disinterested love for them so much as our wishing to live with them and our going to the trouble to learn their language. The *idioma* is usually despised by Spanish-speaking people. The Indians have a feeling that they are looked down upon by people a little higher up in the social scale, and that their language is regarded as an outlandish speech, unworthy of an educated man's attention. I have observed that the Indians of Yatzachi note the contrast between our attitude toward their language, in our desire to learn it, and that of a retired Mexican of Spanish descent in the vicinity, who ridicules the language and, in spite of many years' residence in the village, has learned only absolutely necessary phrases, which he pronounces abominably. His is the typical attitude of Spanish-speaking Mexicans — an attitude of contemptuous superiority. We, on the other hand, want to show our respect for the Indian and for his language. We want him to respect himself and his language, although we also want him to learn Spanish and gradually to substitute Spanish for the *idioma,* in order that he may be assimilated into the Spanish civilization and culture of Mexico, to which, so far, he is practically an outsider. In this connection I wish to quote a passage from a book just published, *The Red Man in the United States,* by Lindquist: ' The American Board reached out to

the lands of the Dakotas, where Doctors Riggs and
Williamson translated the first and, with one exception, the only complete Bible for the Indians
of the United States. Some simple textbooks, de-
votional works, and hymn books were also translated into Dakota, and many of the tribe were
taught to read and write in their own language.
" It is impossible," said Bulletin Number 30 of
the Bureau of American Ethnology, " to estimate
the effect this acquisition has had in stimulating the
self-respect and ambition of the tribe." ' There are
then two elements of the situation, entirely aside
from the reasons based on the importance of giving
the Bible to the Indians in their language: First,
we shall be demonstrating our deep personal interest in the Indians by going to them and learning
their language and living, according to our ability,
a sacrificial life among them, making ourselves ' all
things to all men,' as Paul put it; and second, we
will be teaching them self-respect and ambition by
respecting them and by teaching them new ideals
of home and village life. We firmly believe, also,
that thus approaching them in their own language,
meeting them more than halfway, will have the
effect of making them more desirous of all we have
to teach them, including Spanish, and that instead
of postponing their induction into Spanish civilization, it will hasten it. This is a matter of faith, but
we believe it is based on sound principles.

" A word as to the ideas we have at present in
regard to this language work. There may be some
book or books dealing with the language, but we

have not found them as yet. Probably our best plan is the one which we have followed so far, a purely inductive study, with the help of the men who know Spanish and with the help of one of the most promising of our Protestant converts, a student in Coyoacán. We have formulated a small number of the rules of grammar and forms, and written down quite a vocabulary. We will have to decide on some system of representing the sounds. Quite a few of the sounds resemble sounds in English, such as *sh, z* as in azure, and so forth. The language has tones a little like those in Chinese and Siamese, although they are simpler, and these will have to be represented in some simple way. Some Catholic translations of the catechism, the mass, and certain other ceremonies exist, as well as a large number of titles and deeds of inheritance in the *idioma* of this part of the Sierra, but relatively few people can read these, partly because the form of the language is rather archaic, and partly because they do not understand the system of representing sounds. Consequently we will have to invent or choose a system of phonetic representation of the language, and then teach it to those who already know how to read Spanish. We will do this with our colporteurs and preachers, and with those members of our congregations who can read. We may include this as part of the work in our schools of the future, not allowing it in the slightest degree to displace the learning of Spanish. Workers will have parts of the Bible, translated as carefully as possible, which they can learn by heart, or read, and teach to those who cannot read. Think of the power of such verses as John 3:16 learned by heart by hundreds of Indians, and repeated and explained and illustrated in our services. I believe that the Word of God is literally to-day, as in the days of the apostles, ' living, and active, and sharper than any two-edged sword, and piercing even to the dividing of soul and spirit, of both joints and marrow, and quick to discern the thoughts and intents of the heart.' I trust to the power of the gospel in the native tongue more than I do to the preaching of missionary or of native evangelist.

" We feel that if the program we have in mind can be carried out, it will, under God, be the means of the evangelization of the Sierra in this generation. If we wait for native workers to receive adequate training, and try to supervise them at long distance, the realization of our purpose of evangelization will be postponed fifty years. And we have not all the time in the world at our disposal. The Catholic Church is waking up, and is going to tighten its grip on the Indian if we do not get busy. The government is planning to give far more attention than ever before to schools for the Indians, and unless we can furnish Christian teachers for these schools, we will miss an invaluable opportunity.

" We feel that the training of young Indian men to be the teachers of their people is a vital part of the program of evangelization, but we do not feel that it alone, with occasional visits from the missionary, would be at all adequate. We have several backward congregations in the Mixtecan field that are the result of this type of work, work carried on at a distance by visits and interpreters. However, no well-trained Indian has as yet, in our own field, gone back to his people with the gospel. The Baptists have one such man in one of the Zapotecan villages in the valley of Tlacolula. He is an ordained minister, a thoroughly trained and consecrated man. But in spite of training and earnestness, because of lack of supervision, he has not been very active, and has accomplished relatively little in comparison to what he might have done if well directed. He has preached the gospel in Spanish, though always conversing with the people in the *idioma*. He needed the visit of a specialist in Indian work to show him the necessity of preaching in the Indian language. At the same time, his work has been far better than nothing, and in the case of language groups of small size, such as the Chinantecos in the northern part of the Sierra, I should favor educating young boys to be sent back to their tribes to work under the supervision of a visiting missionary.

" The following is a general outline of the work we should like to establish and develop in the Sierra, with the center, for the present anyway, at Yatzachi:

" 1. Preaching in the Indian language, all services in Zapotecan; translation of the most important parts of the Bible.

" 2. School for boys of the district, similar to

Telixtlahuaca School; aim toward self-support by means of manual work of pupils; emphasis on agricultural training.

"3. Evangelistic work at week-ends by older boys; gradual evangelization of surrounding villages by means of older boys, colporteurs, and personal visits.

"4. Wider work of evangelization of entire district of Villa Alta, and of neighboring district of Ixtlan.

"5. Girls' primary school, with special work in sewing and cooking.

"6. Simple medical work, with sale of medicines.

"I quote the following from my letter to Mr. Reifsnyder in answer to various questions he had asked about our plan:

"'Yatzachi is a good center. It is healthful, has good climate, good water, good air, is well drained. Around it, within an hour's walk in different directions, is a circle of seven villages, including a town of 2,000 population, the largest of the district. Adding two or three hours more, one includes quite a number of good-sized towns. Our plan is to carry on regular religious work in Yatzachi, learning the language well, doing pastoral work, helping a little in a medical way, visiting near-by towns, gradually training colporteurs to travel widely, training the older boys, as in Coyoacán, for evangelistic work, going with them myself often to make visits, bringing boys from other towns to live with us and get a Protestant education, thus forming the same kind of friendly contacts in many other villages that we have found so helpful in Yatzachi.'

"If in the next twenty-five years, with all justice to the other parts of our great field, it should be possible to assign three other evangelistic missionaries to Indian work in Oaxaca, I would suggest the following distribution:

"1. Serrano Zapotecs, 50,000, one missionary, the undersigned.

"2. Valley Zapotecs, 100,000, one missionary.

"3. Mixtecs, 130,000, one missionary.

"4. Mixes, 35,000, one missionary.

Several other smaller groups could be reached by trained native workers. We are thinking in terms of the whole state and of the language conditions we find here.

"To sum up: It is impossible to build a strong individual Christian life or a strong church life on anything but a real knowledge of the Bible. Such a knowledge can never be given by means of the faulty translations of a relatively ignorant Indian interpreter. The plan is to give the vital parts of the Bible to the workers in their own language so that they can give them to the people, by means of a careful translation, made by the thoroughly trained missionary on the basis of the original and the various translations, and with the constant help of the native men in regard to details of the Indian language. To do this, or anything remotely like it, absolutely necessitates residence among the people. It could never be done while living in the city. I am convinced that such work in their own language will be not only the quickest way of evangelizing the Indians, but also of educating them and teaching them Spanish, and the only sure way of building a strong native Church. The Indians have been neglected until now. No work has been done in their language. Spanish is the language of their conquerors and masters. Until white missionaries take the trouble to learn their language, the Indians will not believe in their disinterestedness and love, and will not unreservedly accept the gospel. We must go directly to them if we want them to come to our Christ.

"We feel very deeply that God has led us steadily and very clearly to this plan and this decision. We have both been drawn powerfully and mysteriously to the Serrano Indian. I had the great privilege of opening the field two years ago, and the congregation in Yatzachi I can call my own in the same sense that Paul called many congregations his own. Almost all the boys in our hostel come from this district. We believe, in all humility, that we have a knack for languages, and sufficient linguistic training to handle the problem. Our heart is in the Indian work as in nothing else, and we earnestly wish to give our whole time and attention to it, without having to attend to a large field including Spanish work and work among Mixtecs, as at present. The Indian is worth the best we have. Everyone who knows the Indians of Oaxaca regards the Serrano Indians as being among the most intelligent and most energetic in the state. There is a special interest in an effort to win to

AN INDIAN CHILD

A ZAPOTECO CHRISTIAN

THE APPEAL OF THE INDIAN

"Occasionally among these Indians . . we see one with eyes and hair of extraordinary beauty, a complexion dark but glowing, with the Indian beauty of teeth like the driven snow" (*p. 3*).

the Protestant religion the same race that produced
Benito Juárez, the great Liberal of Mexico. He
is quoted as having said that Protestantism is the
natural religion for a republic, yet his own district
and his own village are still Catholic. Aside from
this sentimental reason, the fact remains that the
great bulk of the population of the state is Indian;
they will hold back the entire state until they are
evangelized and educated, so that in reality, work
among the Indians is the foundation work in this
state. In the opinion of our Station, more work,
and work of a more sacrificial type than ever before, must be done for the Indians. We regard
our plan as a worth-while experiment based on
sound reasons and experience in other fields. We
ask to be given the opportunity to demonstrate the
power of work done by living among the Indians
and adopting their language, believing that our experience will be of value in other parts of the field
where similar conditions may be found. We have
not come to this decision in any sudden way, rather
it is the crystallization of thoughts and longings
that have been in our minds for two years. We
have thought it through carefully, we have faced
frankly all sorts of difficulties involved in the step,
and we are ready to handle them. We believe that
God has called us clearly to this special work. We
ask the Mission to free us from other work in order
that we may devote our entire time and attention
to it."

In 1923, Mr. and Mrs. Van Slyke went to Yatzachi. They have built a house there and are ac-

tively engaged in pioneer service on behalf of the Indian community. This is the first time in the history of Protestant missions in Mexico that an American couple have given themselves entirely to the service of the non-Spanish-speaking Indians, and many have been following Mr. and Mrs. Van Slyke in thought and in prayer as they have entered upon this venture of faith and love.

With reference to Chiapas, reënforcements have been sent to Mexico in 1924 with the hope that one of the new missionaries may be able to take an active part in the work in that state. Especially is there a need for this because of the retirement of Rev. N. J. Elliott from the Mission.

The Reformed Church in America has rendered outstanding service to the Indians in the United States by means of various Missions conducted in the American Southwest. The work of the late Rev. Walter C. Roe and of Mrs. Roe and of their foster son, Rev. Henry Roe Cloud, is known throughout the United States. There are possibilities that the Reformed Church may desire to extend this service beyond the borders of the United States, and on September 24, 1923, the Presbyterian Board of Foreign Missions officially invited the Reformed Church to coöperate in the work in Chiapas through whatever agency the Reformed Church deems appropriate.

This matter is at present under discussion by the Reformed Church and it is hoped that the two Churches may be able to join in this united service on behalf of the Indians of Mexico.

At the meeting of the Foreign Mission Conference in January, 1924, Mr. Legters related an incident taken from his experience in work among the Indians in the United States that applies, as well, to the situation south of the Rio Grande:

" When I was a missionary among the Comanche Indians in the United States, we went to visit Quannah Parker, the last of the great Indian chiefs. As we sat on his porch and talked to him about the gospel we said to him, ' Quannah, what do you think about the gospel?' He said, ' It is good thing for the women and children.' ' But,' we said to him, ' what do you think of it for yourself?' Then he turned and said, ' White man, how long you know this Jesus road?' The missionary said, ' When I was a little boy I knew about it.' He said, ' White man, your father, how long he know about this Jesus road?' ' Why, when my father was a little boy, he knew about this Jesus road.' Then Quannah left the porch and started towards the door. He pulled his blanket around his head and, as he reached the door, he turned and said: ' White man, me heap old man. My heart is turned to stone. You waited too long. You waited too long.' He turned his back to us, and closed the door."

CHAPTER XXI

MISSION DEVELOPMENTS SINCE 1922

SINCE the visit of the Commission to Mexico in the fall of 1922, there have been various developments of interest. A brief summary of the major changes in the various Mission Stations is given in this concluding chapter.

In the Federal District, the sum of $29,000, $25,000 of which was given in memory of Dr. A. W. Halsey, formerly Secretary of the Mexico Mission, has been invested in the Halsey Memorial dormitory building at Coyoacán, and $2,000 has been made available for the social and recreation hall at San Ángel, which was in use as an assembly room for commencement exercises in December, 1924.

Four thousand dollars has been made available for the church and social center in Oaxaca City, and three additional missionaries have been assigned to Oaxaca.

The sum of $2,000 has been appropriated for the church and land at Tapachula, and Chapter XX describes certain measures now being taken to secure more adequate coöperation and assistance from the United States in the work of the Church in Chiapas, and for the Indians in Oaxaca.

In April, 1923, the *Instituto Morelos* in Vera Cruz was closed, chiefly because of the high rent, the lack of permanent property, and the unmet needs of the other schools of the Mission; the American members of the faculty and part of the student body were transferred to the San Ángel School in the Federal District, and the current appropriations were distributed throughout the budget of the Mission.

In August, 1924, the Turner-Hodge School in Mérida purchased permanent property, which, including the cost of organization and the local holding society, cost approximately $41,000.

The property held by the Bible Institute and Social Center in Mérida was also purchased in August, 1924, for approximately $8,000.

The funds for the two latter purchases came from gifts of the 1924 Easter Offering for Mexico of Presbyterian Sunday Schools in the United States and from the Women's Board. There were 1,503 Sunday schools that used the Easter program on Mexico prepared by the Foreign Board, and these schools gave a total of $28,584.05 for the needs in Mexico.

In 1922, the Union Press in Mexico City faced an indebtedness of approximately $16,000. Subsequently, due to the securing of funds by Mr. Day in the United States to clear off this debt, and due to the energy and capacity of Señor Osuna, the local manager, this debt was entirely removed, so that in January, 1924, the Press was clear of all such obligation.

Since the death of Dr. Conwell, the Latin-American hospital at Puebla has been in charge of Dr. Bingham, of the Baptist Mission, and Dr. Illick, of the Methodist Mission; our Mission in 1924 voted to make a contribution for current expenses to the hospital and for the cost of training of hospital nurses of ₱1,000.

When the Commission met with the Mission in December, 1922, a five-year program of property needs was outlined and approved. Some of these needs have already been met. The full list follows:

1. Dormitory, Dining Room for Coyoacán Boys' Preparatory School, Mexico City:
   Total required $65,000.00
   Halsey Memorial Fund assigned and other funds secured 29,000.00
   Balance required $36,000.00
2. Mérida Girls' School, Yucatan, Administration and Dormitory Building:
   Total required 41,000.00
   Already secured 41,000.00
3. Dormitory Equipment for Coyoacán Preparatory School . . 5,000.00
4. Equipment for Mérida Girls' School, Yucatan 5,000.00
5. Coyoacán Missionary Residence 6,000.00
   Already secured 4,571.00
   Balance needed 1,429.00
6. Oaxaca City, Remodeling and Finishing Church Building 7,500.00
   Already secured from Southern Presbyterians 4,062.50
   Balance needed 3,437.50
7. Jalapa, Finish Church Building 1,000.00
8. San Ángel Girls' School Equipment and Gymnasium 7,500.00
   Already secured 2,000.00
   Balance needed 5,500.00
9. Telixtlahuaca, Oaxaca State, Residence and School 4,500.00
   Already secured 1,500.00
   Balance needed 3,000.00
10. Jalapa Property adjacent to Mission for Hostel and Social Work 6,000.00

11.	Oaxaca City, Residence	$6,000.00
12.	Tapachula, Chiapas, Manse	3,000.00
13.	Frontera, Tabasco, Chapel (McCalla Fund)	3,000.00
14.	Coyoacán School Athletic Field	1,500.00
15.	San Ángel, Dormitory Girls' School	30,000.00
	Equipment	5,000.00
16.	Villahermosa, Tabasco, Chapel Manse, and Land	8,000.00
17.	Coyoacán, Mexico City, Pastor's Residence	4,000.00
18.	Muna, Yucatan, Chapel	500.00
19.	Campeche, Campeche, Chapel, Manse and Lot	5,000.00
20.	Missionary Residence, Campeche	5,000.00
21.	Carmen, Campeche, Finish Chapel	1,000.00
22.	Mérida Institutional Work $10,000.00	
	Already secured 8,000.00	
	Balance needed	2,000.00
23.	Puerto Mexico, Vera Cruz, Chapel and Lot	2,000.00
24.	Orizaba Church Remodeling	2,500.00
25.	Vera Cruz Church and Manse	10,000.00
26.	Science Hall for Coyoacán	50,000.00
27.	Mexico City, Morales Memorial Church	12,500.00
28.	San Pedro, San Pablo Chapel and Social Center	12,500.00
29.	Tuxtla Gutiérrez, Chiapas, Chapel and Lot	3,000.00
30.	Two Missionary Residences, Mexico City	18,000.00
31.	Missionary Residence, Mérida	8,000.00
32.	Missionary Residence, Jalapa	8,000.00
33.	Huatusco, Vera Cruz, Chapel and Lot	500.00
34.	Churburná, Yucatan, Chapel	500.00
35.	Sabancuy, Campeche, Chapel	500.00
36.	Tizapan, Mexico City, Social Room	500.00
37.	Tacubaya, Mexico City, Additional Land for Playground	500.00
38.	Tacubaya, Mexico City, Social Equipment	100.00
39.	El Porvenir, Vera Cruz, Chapel	375.00

Since 1922, ten new missionaries have been added to the force in Mexico: Rev. C. H. Ainley, Mr. G. N. Furbeck (on short-term appointment), Rev. and Mrs. G. B. Hammond, Miss Anne C. Hawley, Rev. Paul H. Leavens, Miss M. L. Pitman, Miss L. S. Plummer, Rev. and Mrs. N. W. Taylor. The Mission has suffered heavy losses, however, due to resignation, withdrawal, and death. Nine missionaries have thus retired from the serv-

ice, so that the net gain in Mission membership is only one. Through coöperative agreements, the Mission has been assigned the sole responsibility for Protestant work in one fourth of the territory of Mexico and for one fifth of the population, totaling over three million souls. This field includes six states and one territory, as well as a share in the work in the Federal District. In 1924 there was not a single resident missionary in the states of Chiapas, Tabasco, and Campeche, and in the Territory of Quintana Roo. Such important cities and centers as Vera Cruz, Orizaba, Tapachula, and Tuxtla Gutiérrez were without any missionaries. When the Board accepted the responsibility for this territory in 1914, it stated in its action that at least sixty missionaries would be needed. In 1924 there were thirty-four missionaries on the field. There is need to-day, no less than in 1914, for volunteers who, for Christ's sake, will cross the Rio Grande, to serve those who are our neighbors in his name. The field is there. The need is there. The call is clear and strong. " He that hath ears to hear, let him hear."

A BRIEF READING LIST ON MEXICO

(NOTE. — For those who desire a shorter list than the following, certain books which might be included in such an abbreviated list, are starred.)

HISTORY

* *The Mexican Nation,* by Herbert Priestley. The Macmillan Company, New York, 1923.

A thorough review of the development of the Mexican nation from the earliest known history of the land and its people to the inauguration of President Obregon, with a discussion of some of the perplexing problems of to-day.

Mexico, To-Day and To-Morrow, by E. D. Trowbridge. The Macmillan Company, New York, 1919.

A briefer survey than the preceding book, giving a concise statement of the development of Mexico to 1918.

* *The Conquest of Mexico,* by William H. Prescott (1843). Everyman's Library, E. P. Dutton and Company, New York, 1909. (New Edition, 2 vols.)

A classic which ought to be in the library of everyone interested in Mexico.

SOCIAL AND ECONOMIC DEVELOPMENT

* *The Land Systems of Mexico,* by George M. McBride. American Geographical Society, New York, Research Series No. 12.

The clearest and most comprehensive statement of the agrarian problem in Mexico which has thus far been produced.

* *The Social Revolution in Mexico,* by E. A. Ross. Century Company, New York, 1923.

A brief survey and estimate of recent developments in Mexico, written by a well-known sociologist and observer.

Mexico, An Interpretation, by Carleton Beals. B. W. Buebsch, New York, 1923.

A frank discussion of present conditions and tendencies in Mexico. With many of the author's statements there will undoubtedly be disagreement, but his views are informative and challenging, and will provoke further study nd investigation.

DESCRIPTION

* 's *Mexico,* by T. Terry. New Edition, 1923. ghton Mifflin Company, New York.

standard guidebook to Mexico which is full of valu- information.

In t of El Dorado, by Stephen Graham. D. Appleton ompany, New York, 1923.

interesting description of present-day Mexico t the background of Spain, the West Indies, New , and Panama.

A G in Mañana-Land, by Harry L. Foster. Dodd, M nd Company, New York, 1924.

adable narrative giving the author's impressions of co and the Central American Republics.

*Mexic Frank G. Carpenter. Doubleday, Page and Company, w York, 1924.

One of the volumes in the series of "Carpenter's World Travels." Superficial but of value in giving initial impressions of the people and the country.

Beautiful Mexico — Its Stories, Legends and Scenic Charm, by Vernon Quinn. Frederick A. Stokes Company, New York, 1924.

This book emphasizes the picturesque and attractive aspects of the Mexican landscape and the Mexican people.

In an Unknown Land, by Thomas Gann. Charles Scribner's Sons, New York, 1924.

A description of an expedition through Yucatan by representatives of the Maya Society and the Carnegie Institute, which has brought to light new and interesting information concerning the little-known and ancient cities of this portion of Mexico.

Mexican Year Book for 1922–1924 — Edited by Robert G. Cleland.   Los Angeles Times-Mirror Press — 1924.

The second volume of these year books, which have already won for themselves a distinct place as an authoritative compendium of current information concerning Mexico.

RELIGIONS OF MEXICO

The Gods of Mexico, by Lewis Spence.   Frederick A. Stokes Company, New York, 1923.

A thorough and authoritative study of the religions of the peoples of ancient Mexico, illustrated for the most part from native paintings and pottery.

Roman Christianity in Latin America, by Webster E. Browning.   Fleming H. Revell and Company, New York, 1924.

One of the volumes in the " Living Religions " series. A clear, succinct summary of Roman Catholicism in Latin America from the Protestant viewpoint by one who has lived and worked for twenty-eight years in South America.

PROTESTANT WORK

Mexico To-Day, by George B. Winton.   Missionary Education Movement, New York, 1916.

A brief survey of the situation which, although not up to date, still has a distinct value.

FICTION

Montezuma's Daughter, by H. Rider Haggard.   Longmans Green Company, New York.

The scenes of this novel are laid in the capital of Mexico during the last days of the rule of the Montezumas and their conquest by the Spaniards.

The current publications of the Pan American Union, Washington, D.C., also contain much of information and interest concerning Mexico.